CRIMINAL INVESTIGATION

THE PROFESSIONAL POLICING CURRICULUM IN PRACTICE

IAIN STAINTON AND ROBERT EWIN
SERIES EDITOR: TONY BLOCKLEY

CRITICAL PUBLISHING

First published in 2022 by Critical Publishing Ltd

All rights reserved. No part of this publication may be reproduced, stored in a retrieval system, or transmitted in any form or by any means, electronic, mechanical, photocopying, recording or otherwise, without prior permission in writing from the publisher.

The authors have made every effort to ensure the accuracy of information contained in this publication, but assume no responsibility for any errors, inaccuracies, inconsistencies and omissions. Likewise, every effort has been made to contact copyright holders. If any copyright material has been reproduced unwittingly and without permission the Publisher will gladly receive information enabling them to rectify any error or omission in subsequent editions.

Copyright © 2022 Iain Stainton and Robert Ewin

British Library Cataloguing in Publication Data
A CIP record for this book is available from the British Library

ISBN: 978-1-914171-50-5

This book is also available in the following e-book formats:
EPUB ISBN: 978-1-914171-51-2
Adobe e-book ISBN: 978-1-914171-52-9

The rights of Robert Ewin and Iain Stainton to be identified as the Authors of this work have been asserted by them in accordance with the Copyright, Design and Patents Act 1988.

Cover and text design by Out of House Limited
Project management by Newgen Publishing UK
Printed and bound in Great Britain by 4edge, Essex

To order, or for details of our bulk discounts, please go to our website www.criticalpublishing.com or contact our distributor, Ingram Publisher Services (IPS UK), 10 Thornbury Road, Plymouth PL6 7PP, telephone 01752 202301 or email IPSUK.orders@ingramcontent.com.

Critical Publishing
3 Connaught Road
St Albans
AL3 5RX

www.criticalpublishing.com

PAPER FROM
RESPONSIBLE
SOURCES

CONTENTS

About the series editor and authors	iv
Foreword by the series editor	v
Acknowledgements	vi
Chapter 1: Introduction to the investigative process	1
Chapter 2: Key principles of criminal investigation	17
Chapter 3: Investigative practice	39
Chapter 4: Witness and victim management	63
Chapter 5: Investigative interviewing	83
Chapter 6: Specialist support	107
Chapter 7: Covert methods	127
Chapter 8: Complex cases	145
Chapter 9: Measuring investigative success	163
Sample answers	183
References	189
Index	205

ABOUT THE SERIES EDITOR

TONY BLOCKLEY

is the lead for policing at the University of Derby, responsible for co-ordinating policing higher education, including developing programmes and enhancing the current provision in line with the Police Education Qualifications Framework (PEQF) and supporting the College of Policing. He served within policing for over 30 years, including a role as Chief Superintendent and Head of Crime.

ABOUT THE AUTHORS

ROBERT EWIN

is a serving police officer, practitioner and researcher whose main interests include the psychology of mindlessness, investigative practices relating to witnesses and policing responses to vulnerable populations. He currently leads the delivery of new police officer and specialist investigation training alongside the PEQF.

IAIN STAINTON

is a senior lecturer in security, intelligence and investigative practice at the University of Cumbria. He has over 30 years' practical policing experience in a variety of overt and covert investigative roles.

FOREWORD

Police professionalism has seen significant developments over recent years, including the implementation of the Vision 2025 and the establishment of the Police Education Qualifications Framework (PEQF). There is no doubt that policing has become complex, and that complexity and associated challenges increase day by day with greater scrutiny, expectation and accountability. The educational component of police training and development therefore allows officers to gain a greater understanding and appreciation of the theories and activities associated with high-quality policing provision.

The scholastic element of the Vision 2025 provides opportunity to engage in meaningful insight and debate around some of the most sensitive areas of policing while also taking the lessons of the past and utilising them to develop the service for the future. While there are many books and articles on numerous subjects associated with policing, this new series – *The Professional Policing Curriculum in Practice* – provides an insightful opportunity to start that journey. It distils the key concepts and topics within policing into an accessible format, combining theory and practice, to provide you with a secure basis of knowledge and understanding.

With policing now a degree-level entry profession, this has provided a unique opportunity to develop fully up-to-date books for student and trainee police officers that focus on the content of the PEQF curriculum, are tailored specifically to the new pre-join routes, and reflect the diversity and complexity of twenty-first-century society. Each book is stand-alone, but they also work together to layer information as you progress through your programme. The pedagogical features of the books have been carefully designed to improve your understanding and critical thinking skills within the context of policing. They include learning objectives, case studies, evidence-based practice examples, critical thinking and reflective activities, and summaries of key concepts. Each chapter also includes a guide to further reading, meaning you don't have to spend hours researching to find that piece of information you are looking for.

In this first book in the series, *Criminal Investigation*, authors Iain Stainton and Rob Ewin use their extensive knowledge and experience to focus on the history, background and development of criminal investigations before moving on to some of the key principles, investigative practice, and engaging witnesses and suspects. They examine the specialist support available to investigators and consider the challenges of complex cases.

Having been involved in policing for over 40 years, the benefits of these books are obvious to me: I see them becoming the go-to guides for the PEQF curriculum across all the various programmes associated with the framework while also having relevance for more experienced officers.

Tony Blockley
Discipline Head: Policing
University of Derby

ACKNOWLEDGEMENTS

I would like to recognise the part colleagues, victims, witnesses, students and offenders, too numerous to mention, have all played in creating the memories and experiences that have inspired this book.

Thanks to Becky and Sarah for their expertise and limitless patience in supporting us from origin to completion.

Most importantly, Mrs S, your unquestioning support across many years and two careers can finally be recognised in print. Thanks, Shaz, we have got our weekends back (until the next project!).

Iain Stainton

Writing a book for policing studies is not an easy task, and I'd like to thank all those students within Cumbria Constabulary whose feedback has added value to this project and who help shape the future relationship between knowledge and operational skills. You do an amazing job in balancing your studies and working lives with the expectations of victims, suspects and the organisation. I hope this book serves you well in your careers as a useful starting point for knowledge.

My retired police dog, Merlin, has been equally helpful, dragging me away from my desk for fresh air. So thanks must also go to him. And, without hesitation or doubt, thanks to Iain Stainton for his wonderfully energetic enthusiasm for the topic.

Rob Ewin

CHAPTER 1
INTRODUCTION TO THE INVESTIGATIVE PROCESS

LEARNING OBJECTIVES

AFTER READING THIS CHAPTER YOU WILL BE ABLE TO:

- outline the history of criminal investigation;
- summarise the influence of practice on legislation and police powers;
- relate crime management and statistics to the public fear of crime;
- demonstrate a critical understanding of the Volume Crime Management Model.

INTRODUCTION

Criminal investigation is a core element of policing. Mission statements and objectives ranging from counter-terrorism to anti-social behaviour and quality of life issues would be unachievable without investigative skills.

Any examination of the media ranging from news to entertainment will verify the place of criminal investigation in the public's consciousness. Fictional characters such as Sherlock Holmes and Inspector Morse portray investigators as maverick, intuitive individuals who rarely fail to solve crimes as a result of their intelligent approach, contributing to the popularist view of 'the detective' as an artisan. This gives rise to the art, craft or science debate (Tong et al, 2009; O'Neill, 2018), which will be explored in this chapter.

Crime and criminal behaviour affects people across society. The Telephone-operated Crime Survey for England and Wales (TCSEW; Office for National Statistics 2020) estimate that 9.7 million adults experienced being a victim of crime in 2019–20. Enquiries into events such as the death of Stephen Lawrence (1993) confirm the public's desire for professional, competent investigators to enquire into matters on their behalf.

This book divides criminal investigation into specific elements, which when combined will contribute to your mastery of the practice. Understanding origins leads to heightened comprehension which means we start with the history of 'the detective'. This opening chapter then uncovers links between practice and evolving legislation. Explanations are accentuated through policing spotlight sections and your engagement with the material is encouraged with reflective and critical activities throughout.

HISTORY

The origins of contemporary policing can be traced to the establishment of the Metropolitan Police in 1829. There were public suspicions of the new police, together with a continental influence where the police were viewed as spies, while forerunners such as the Bow Street Runners had a reputation as a mercenary group of thief catchers known for their poor and corrupt practice (O'Neill, 2018). These factors contributed to the decision not to establish a detective branch at this point, which was a situation that remained unchanged until the introduction of a small 'plain clothes' department to investigate crime in 1842. It would be a further 36 years before a recognisable Criminal Investigation Department (CID) was established in 1878, with a specialised counter-terrorism unit known as 'Special Investigation Branch' or Special Branch following in 1884 to counteract a growing terrorist threat.

CRITICAL THINKING ACTIVITY 1.1

LEVEL 4

Investigative specialisms develop in response to policing challenges. Make a list of contemporary specialties in policing where detectives concentrate on distinct crime types and then consider what led to these specialist departments becoming established.

The 1919 Desborough Committee of enquiry into policing suggested that detectives required no additional training; any essential ability would be acquired through experience in a practical environment. Interpretations suggesting that detective skills were possessed rather than learnt supported the portrayal of fictional investigators as gifted individuals honing their inherent art and supporting less gifted officers. This was a predominant situation for some time, supported by studies such as that by the Rand Corporation (1975), which suggested that members of the public contributed the majority of crime-solving material rather than investigators discovering it.

The 1970s corruption probes of Sir Robert Mark, combined with revelations of bad practice through the Birmingham Six (1975) and Guildford Four (1975) enquiries, served to focus a lens on the detective role. Criticisms about corruption and bias rightly attract the most attention. The origins of the Police and Criminal Evidence Act 1984 (PACE), one of the most significant pieces of legislation you will encounter, can be traced to events such as the Brixton riots and miners' strike of the early 1980s. A closer examination reveals a thread of poor decision making, lack of aligning intelligence with investigation, and inadequate management to be present where detectives' actions fall below the public's expectations. The identified lack of skills in investigative practice led to the establishment of the Professionalising Investigation Programme (PIP) in 2005, accompanied by the introduction of *Practice Advice on Core Investigative Doctrine* (CD) in 2012 and the *Murder Investigation Manual* (MIM) in 2006, providing practitioners with key principles to support their decision making. The need for a comprehensive national training system was recognised. PIP was created to address investigation from junior to senior positions in the police, and provided the origins for current practice.

PROFESSIONALISING INVESTIGATIONS

With CD and MIM providing the foundations, PIP was sub-divided into four levels (see Figure 1.1) to ensure relevance of knowledge and understanding to specific roles. An important aspect of the programme was the realisation that continuous professional development is integral to professionalism.

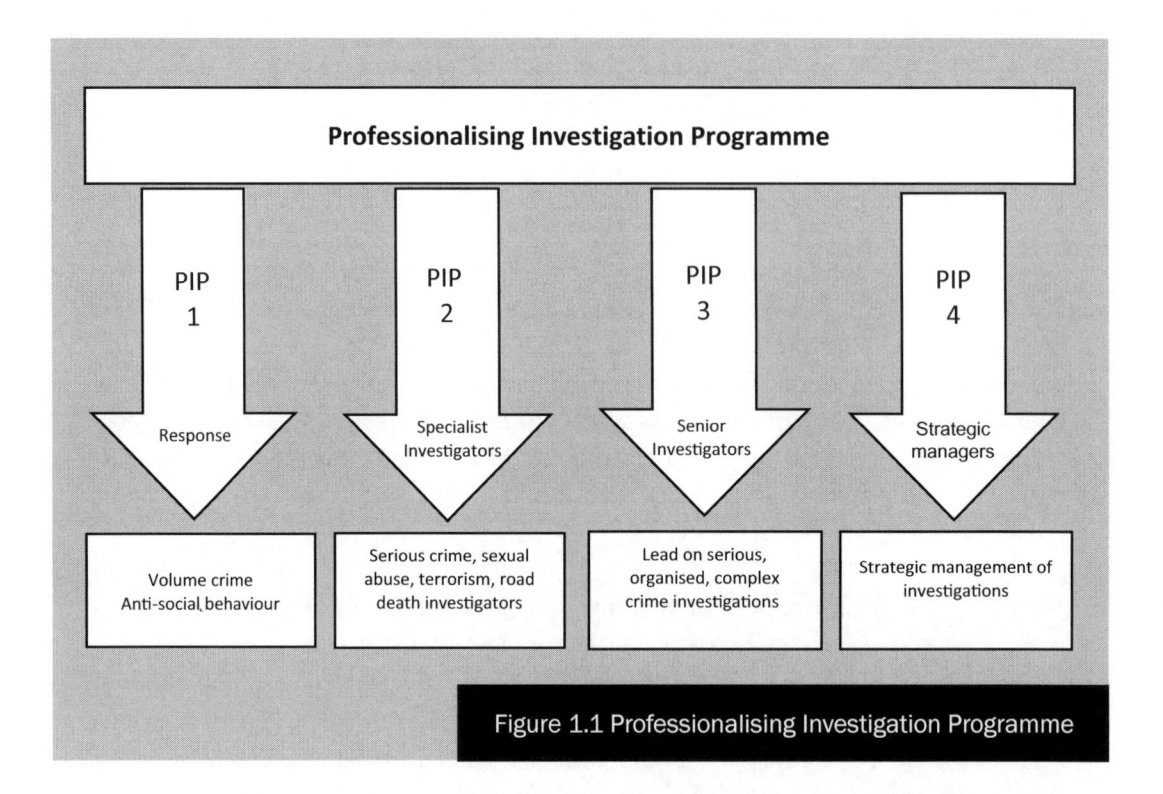

Figure 1.1 Professionalising Investigation Programme

PIP combined classroom learning with officers demonstrating competencies in a practical environment, evidenced in portfolios and assessed against national occupational standards which specified a series of competencies that the investigator must possess:

- decision making;

- leadership;

- professionalism;

- working with others.

The programme established a skill base across policing, with level 1 ensuring a fundamental competency in initial incident response and interview techniques. Level 2 addressed the need for initial management of incidents, embedding investigative knowledge and skills appropriate to serious and complex crimes, while level 3 provided material specifically for senior investigating officers (SIOs). The strategic importance of investigations was addressed through level 4, ensuring senior managers had the requisite skills.

PIP led to some of the first partnerships between policing and academia, where elements of the training were accredited to count towards higher education qualifications, for example in Kent 2001–06 and Cumbria 2009–10.

PIP recognised that criminal investigation is a specific skill, requiring investment in time and expertise to meet the needs of society and policing, while equipping officers to meet these needs. PIP represented a widening of skill bases with previously detective-specific training becoming available to officers from a variety of other roles who would benefit from investigative skills.

Historical investigative training concentrated on providing knowledge of substantive law, relying on the craft element to embed this knowledge with practical competence into the workplace environment. This unstructured approach was dependent on many variables, including the approach of peers, the experiences encountered and the workplace environment itself. This created an unaccountable, subjective approach to investigators' capability. Aligning understanding of the knowledge elements with extending training into the workplace allowed investigators to develop legislative knowledge of both substantive and procedural law. This extended to influences such as the very existence of legal frameworks, enabling practice to meet the expectations of both the police and the public.

The current Police Education Qualifications Framework (PEQF) partnerships between policing and higher education represent the current evolution of a professionalisation agenda. As noted earlier in the chapter, investigative training used to be dominated by a focus on law. It is essential to recognise that an understanding of law should be complemented by practice. Continuing the theme of starting with the origins of the investigative process, the next section will outline how practice influences law.

POWERS AND LEGISLATION

Roberts (2007) notes that legislation influences criminal investigations in two ways: by clarifying specific objectives and regulating the actions of the investigator. Historical investigative training concentrated on providing a knowledge of law at the expense of practice. However, Roberts' two objectives can be achieved in the nexus between learning and the workplace.

Traditionally investigators react to reports of criminal behaviour, and it is unlikely that the originator of the report will identify which offence has been committed. One of your first steps will be to identify which, if any, criminal offence has occurred. You will often hear the phrase 'points to prove'. This refers to an analysis of law, identifying elements that your investigation will need to achieve to support a successful prosecution.

POLICING SPOTLIGHT

Imagine you are an operational officer encountering an allegation of theft. Section 1 of the Theft Act 1968 defines the offence as follows.

A person is guilty of theft if he dishonestly appropriates property belonging to another with the intention of permanently depriving the other of it.

Sections 2–6 of the act define the 'points to prove' as:

1. dishonesty;

2. appropriation;

3. property;

4. belonging to another;

5. intention to permanently deprive.

As an investigator seeking to prove the offence you must ensure all these elements are present. Some may be demonstrated through investigation, some by interview. Drawing the elements together to confirm the commission of an offence is indictive of a professional investigation.

During an investigation you will consider a range of tactical options as outlined in the following chapters. Many require you to have knowledge supportive powers provided by law such as search or arrest. Procedural law (see Table 1.1) provides a legal framework to your choices, which must be satisfied before action is taken. Procedural legislation defines people's rights and confirms the integrity of investigative material obtained. Table 1.1 lists key legislation in an investigative setting (please note that this is an indicative rather than an exhaustive list).

Table 1.1 Permissive legislation

Legislation	Significance
Police and Criminal Evidence Act 1984	Police powers; suspect and public rights
Criminal Procedure and Investigations Act 1996	Defines investigation and legislates for neutrality. Provides disclosure rules
Human Rights Act 1998	Creates absolute, qualified and limited rights and the associated duty to protect these rights
Regulation of Investigatory Powers Act 2000	Framework for investigative practice in communications and surveillance approaches
Serious Organised Crime and Police Act 2005	Amends powers of arrest

The aim of the police is to prevent crime, and traditionally investigators react to reports of criminal behaviour. The criminal behaviour, punishments and the powers used in an investigation are defined by law, which evolves over time in line with societal conditions. Thankfully, stealing a rabbit is no longer punishable with deportation as it was in the 1830s. Police practice is regularly seen as influencing law through 'case law'. Identification issues defined in *R v Turnbull and Camelo* [1977] are known to most officers as the 'Turnbull rules' or by the mnemonic ADVOKATE.

- **A**mount or length of time under observation.

- **D**istance between observer and person observed.

- **V**isibility conditions at the time.

- **O**bstructions to view.

- **K**nown to observer.

- **A**ny reason for remembering.

- **T**ime under observation.

- **E**rrors between description and actual appearance.

EVIDENCE-BASED POLICING

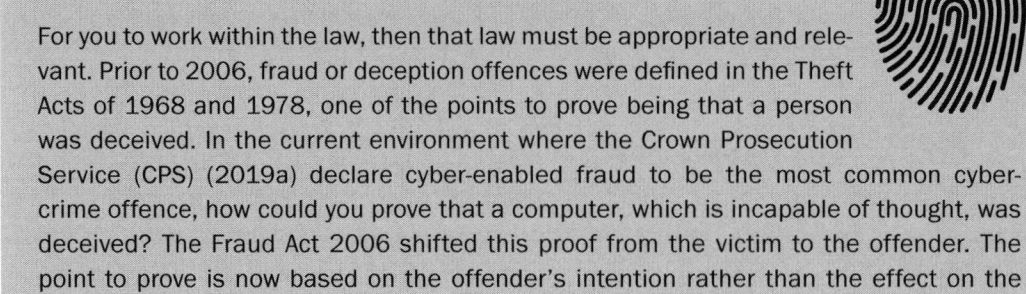

For you to work within the law, then that law must be appropriate and relevant. Prior to 2006, fraud or deception offences were defined in the Theft Acts of 1968 and 1978, one of the points to prove being that a person was deceived. In the current environment where the Crown Prosecution Service (CPS) (2019a) declare cyber-enabled fraud to be the most common cybercrime offence, how could you prove that a computer, which is incapable of thought, was deceived? The Fraud Act 2006 shifted this proof from the victim to the offender. The point to prove is now based on the offender's intention rather than the effect on the victim. This is an example of the evolution of legislation to meet the needs of the time.

The inquisitorial justice system of the United Kingdom requires investigators to conduct their enquiries without bias, following all leads without prejudice. This is a condition known as the investigative mindset, which is further examined in Chapter 2. The legislation identified in Table 1.1 requires in-depth understanding in order to apply this mindset in a practical environment.

Neyroud and Beckley (2001, pp 9–10) suggest that policing exists in a series of 'vicious cycles': concentrating on fighting crime before encountering corruption and scandal, which in turn creates a societal and institutional reaction, leading to new norms or rules before returning to crime fighting. This cause-and-effect relationship can be related to the origins of the Police and Criminal Evidence Act (PACE 1984), which may be traced to a series of miscarriages of justice, such as the aforementioned Birmingham Six (1975) and Guildford Four (1975) and poor practice in the adoption of stop and search practices, which the 1981 Scarman report confirmed to be a key factor in the 1981 Brixton riots. Scarman made a series of recommendations regarding training and law: the introduction of PACE, arguably the major legislative influence on modern-day policing, was a direct result of these recommendations. Enquiries into practice, such as the Byford review (1981) into the Yorkshire Ripper investigation, led to the establishment of the Home Office Large Major Enquiry System (HOLMES), one of the foundational information technology (IT) systems to support investigative practice. In a common law jurisdiction, such as the UK, legislation can be confused by a multitude of stated cases over time. Clarification such as that provided by the Criminal Procedure and Investigations Act 1996 is welcome to address a situation. In the case of the Regulation of Investigatory Powers Act 2000 (RIPA), surveillance and informants had been used in investigations for many years prior to 2000, governed by policy rather than legislation. The introduction of the Human Rights Act 1998 created a series of rights. Certain ones may be breached providing this is 'in accordance with law' (Chapter 7 explores this in detail). RIPA legislated for such practices to ensure such practices were human rights compliant: a situation to be welcomed. There is now law authorising these practices rather than less precise guidance or policy.

Knowledge and understanding of law must be organic and continuous: since an investigator's career can last many years and encounter many changes, it is incumbent on you to maintain your knowledge and understanding. Most people's personal experience of investigation will unfortunately arise from being a victim of crime. The opportunity to create an impression is a valuable opportunity. This chapter will now move on to volume crime, which represents the majority of victims' experiences.

> ## CRITICAL THINKING ACTIVITY 1.2
> ### LEVEL 5
>
> As a policing student you will be familiar with current practice and policy. Summarise any areas of policing you believe would benefit from a re-imagining of police powers or legislation.

VOLUME CRIME

Reporting of criminal investigations centres on dramatic, newsworthy events. Fictional detectives are always associated with serious crimes. However, the impact of actual crime is most keenly felt by victims of volume crime.

Volume crime is traditionally associated with robbery, burglary, theft, damage, drug offences and assaults. The Association of Chief Police Officers (ACPO) (2009, p 8) defines volume crime '*as any crime which through its sheer volume, has a significant impact on the community and the ability of the police to tackle it*'. This wide-ranging definition commonly includes offences such as burglary, theft, drugs or assault, and emphasises the difficult relationship between events and perception. The perception that volume crime is of lesser importance is discussed below, while the fact that it has a significant impact is addressed in the above definition. It is vital that victims believe their situation merits attention since failing to achieve this has the potential to undermine police–community relations. Collectively, volume crime accounts for the majority of recorded crime. Brown and Smith (2018) confirm that while volume crime offences have relatively low clearance rates, they are identified as a priority among members of the public.

The influence of investigative practice on law and policy can be appreciated by examining the origins of the Volume Crime Management Model (VCMM) (NPIA, 2009), attributable to the public impact and the paucity of detection of such offences. VCMM is a triage-based screening approach starting with the initial report. As will be seen in Chapter 2, the acquisition of material at an early stage is essential to any investigation. The model requires call handlers to maximise and analyse the information obtained to decide if the investigation is likely to benefit from an officer's attendance, introducing a selective process where investigators are deployed where they will be most efficient. Under the terms of VCMM, not all crimes will merit the attendance of an investigator. This screening process continues throughout the initial stages as information is sought and acted upon, incrementally influencing the attendance of specialists such as crime scene investigators. If it is believed that nothing useful can be gained, the investigation can be closed. This discretionary approach to criminal investigation places responsibility on those at each stage of the investigation to gather material professionally, analysing the information to support decision making in accordance with an open-minded investigative mindset. This procedural approach is unique to volume crime investigations, and a more contextual approach is encouraged in major crime enquiries.

The credibility of the screening approach is provided by Eck's (1979) study, suggesting that crime screening accurately predicts the result of an investigation in excess of 80 per cent of the cases analysed. The Metropolitan Police policy on crime screening refers to the effect on victims and communities of the offence and the decision to effectively cease the investigation (Metropolitan Police, 2017). This equation is included in the decision to screen crimes, aligning with a move to recognise the place of the victim in criminal justice, demonstrated by the development of the Victim Code (MoJ, 2020).

Victim satisfaction is an important aspect of the relationship between the police and the public; as with any service, perceived poor service has a detrimental effect on trust. Myhill and Bradford (2012) explore the phenomenon of victim satisfaction being more reliant on the perception of the investigation than its success. Where there is a perception of an investigation being based on prioritising resources and efficiency rather than effectiveness, the danger of eroding public confidence and support will be ever present. The following policing spotlight and reflective practice activity encourage you to explore this further.

POLICING SPOTLIGHT

Put yourself in the position of a victim of crime. Imagine your vehicle is stolen, the type of volume crime offence investigators deal with daily. Recognise the impact this event would have on you: losing not only your mode of transport but also the vehicle contents, personal items, mementos and private articles. Would you feel intruded upon?

This invasion of self happens to all victims of crime. Placing yourself in the victim's shoes will be chastening and influential on your practice.

REFLECTIVE PRACTICE 1.1

LEVEL 5

As a professional investigator you will prioritise victim and witness care in serious cases, as demonstrated in Chapters 8 and 9. Reflect on your dealings with 'volume crimes' and be alert for signs of distress. It may be a familiar scenario for you to investigate but could be a significant event in the life of your victim.

People's perceptions of crime are based on many more variables than experience. You will encounter and be asked to counter this 'fear of crime'; it is therefore important that you are aware of the contributing influences.

IMPRESSIONS OF CRIMINALITY

As a policing student you are probably immersed in a policing environment, and as such are exposed to police work and wider associated news stories on a daily basis. This is a unique situation since the majority of people assess police effectiveness through personal experience, media and statistics. Statistically, the public are most likely to encounter volume crime. The influence of the media on fear of crime will be explored in Chapter 8. Crime statistics feature in and generate media exposure, which in turn prompts public reaction. These combine to influence confidence in the investigative response, a vital element of any investigation addressing the willingness of people to contribute. A lack of engagement between the public and policing may result in decisions not to report crime. This is a situation Professor Jonathan Shepherd (2015) suggests contributes to recorded crime figures only representing between 40 and 60 per cent of actual crime.

The implications of recorded crime not presenting a true picture are significant across a range of societal issues, not least the fear and perception of being a victim of crime. The Home Office introduced the National Crime Recording Standards in 2002 to standardise recording criteria. The current recording rules (2021) highlight a victim focus through the following principle.

> *The Standard directs a victim focused approach to crime recording. The intention is that victims are believed and benefit from statutory entitlements under the Code of Practice for Victims of Crime (CPVC). This seeks to ensure that those reporting crimes will be treated with empathy and their allegations will be taken seriously. Any investigation which follows is then taken forward with an open mind to establish the truth.*
>
> (Home Office, 2021, p 3)

The crime statistics picture is informed by two distinct surveys: police recorded crime and the Telephone-operated Crime Survey for England and Wales (TCSEW), previously Crime Survey for England and Wales. Police record crime in accordance with Home Office counting rules which mandate which crimes are recorded. TCSEW estimates instances of crime using a research methodology. A statistical disparity between these surveys prompts questions being asked regarding their accuracy.

The recording of crime is dependent upon the event being recorded by the police; Chapter 8 examines whether crime statistics are representative of the true situation. Influencing factors such as trust, an opinion that little will be achieved, intimidation or lack of understanding may affect reports being made. Police recorded crime is dependent on discretion, as officers decide if an event amounts to a recordable crime upon receipt of the initial report (detected crime statistics also feature in this database, which will be further examined in Chapter 9). Home Office counting rules discount some crimes, such as anti-social behaviour, from recorded statistics. Other statistics such as drug offences are heavily influenced by police activity rather than actual criminality. A 2014 report by Her Majesty's Inspectorate of Constabulary and Fire & Rescue Services (HMICFRS) revealed that only 80 per cent of reported offences were correctly recorded (HMICFRS, 2014, p 46), a situation giving rise to the Office for National Statistics (2020) declaring they do not currently meet the criteria to be classified as national statistics.

TCSEW estimates crime rates from a sample population survey of adults over 18 years of age. It analyses information from 'households', meaning that offences targeted at business or those not resident in a 'household' are not calculated. 'Victimless' crimes such as drugs offences do not feature in TCSEW. Less common crimes are prone to misrepresentative figures.

Reviewing the above, you can see that it is difficult to draw conclusions without further analysis into the trends and themes, which most people are unlikely to pursue. Where, then, will people gather their information from about the prevalence of crime? Trustworthy sources include personal experiences, friends, family, community, news and social media. Mainstream sources tend to be 'echo chambers' of a person's profile: their social circle, including social media, tends towards people who share views and opinions, and people choose entertainment and news media based on personal preferences. It is unlikely any of these will provide critical discussion of the type you would experience in a student seminar. People's fear of crime rarely reflects actual crime. Grinshteyn (2013) confirms that people are not very good at determining the real risk of crime; the perception that they will be victim of a crime is not based on statistics or probability. The fear of crime phenomenon influences behaviours in personal and social contexts, affecting both people and locations. Citizens become protective and withdraw from perceived dangerous environments. Locations may be viewed as 'no-go' areas. Relationships with other individuals or groups (including police) can be viewed as unwise. These very real situations can be associated with volume crime as much as serious or serial offending.

> **REFLECTIVE PRACTICE 1.2**
>
> **LEVEL 6**
>
> Ferraro (1995) defines fear of crime as an emotional response of dread and anxiety to symbols associated with crime. Analyse your interpretation of violent crime compared to crime statistics, and then identify the sources that accord with your view. Why do these sources portray crime in this manner? As an investigator how can you combat this?

The importance of perception of crime is discernible from the political attention it attracts. From the 'tough on crime, tough on the causes of crime' speech of the then Prime Minister, Tony Blair (1995), which preceded a series of justice system reforms, to the Police, Crime, Sentencing and Courts Bill (2021) proposals to increase sentencing powers, alongside investments in developing TCSEW by successive governments, politicians recognise the importance of society feeling secure. The public perception of becoming a victim of crime does not align with the likelihood of becoming a victim. The 2016 Crime Survey of England and Wales (CSEW) (Office for National Statistics, 2016) revealed that 20 per cent of the adult population believed they were fairly or very likely to be a victim of crime, which is a figure consistent with that from previous years; conversely, the same survey confirmed that less than 10 per cent of the population did experience crime as a victim. Gillespie and McLaughlin's 2002 research on the role of the media in shaping public attitudes suggests that personal experiences can shape the normally predominant media influence, confirming the importance of professional practice in environments beyond that of the crime itself.

According to Hancock (2004), rationalising society's perception of crime is a crucial factor in engaging the public, maintaining legitimacy and enabling strategic planning, all of which are vital in the police–public relationship. Home Office crime surveys categorise fear of crime by gender, location and ethnicity to provide specific information that can support a targeted approach in a style advocated by the National Intelligence Model. In an attempt to ensure communities have access to up-to-date information about the state of criminality in their community area, local crime statistics are now available through Police.UK web pages.

CONCLUSION

This chapter has unpacked the history of investigative practice, explaining how the drive to professionalise practice contributed to current approaches. It has shown how investigative practice addresses crime and criminality, shapes legislation, and guides the public's relationship with policing and their perception of crime. In short, the chapter has touched on a diverse range of issues.

Scrutiny of policy in respect of volume crime emphasises the link between public perceptions and investigators as 'front of house' representatives of the police.

Considerations regarding fear of crime reveal how the involvement of the general public in the criminal justice system creates an information exchange environment that contributes to a more informed understanding of policing and criminal justice matters. This is imperative in maintaining trust and support in investigative processes. This process pivots on the impressions you create through your role as an investigator.

The Police Education Qualifications Framework (PEQF) and Detective Degree Holder Entry Programmes (DHEP) represent contemporary approaches to ensuring investigators are equipped to face the challenges brought by investigating crime. The historic view of the detective as an artisan of their craft is now universally seen as outdated, which is confirmed by policing degrees now being designated Bachelor of Science (BSc) rather than Bachelor of Arts (BA). This book emphasises the complexity of investigative work and associated competencies where understanding transcends simple knowledge, which has contributed to policing becoming a profession.

SUMMARY OF KEY CONCEPTS

This opening chapter introduces criminal investigation. The content equips you to:

- trace the evolution of criminal investigation;
- relate your learning to professional requirements;
- recognise events which influence professional practice;
- establish connections between law and contemporary investigations;
- summarise the links between crime and public perception.

CHECK YOUR KNOWLEDGE

1. You are a dedicated investigator working on serious sexual offences. Which PIP level do you expect to be qualified to? Which PIP level will your senior investigating officer (SIO) manager be qualified to?

2. You are investigating a report of a crime. The offender has climbed through an open window into the staff room of a local shop. They were disturbed by a member of staff while searching staff lockers and ran away through the shop. Money and phones were found to be missing from the lockers. What offence have you identified?

3. What are the 'points to prove' in the above offence you have identified?

4. The offence is one in a series of incidents. How will you address the local community's 'fear of crime'?

Sample answers to these questions are provided at the end of the book.

FURTHER READING

Neyroud, P and Beckley, A (2001) *Policing, Ethics and Human Rights*. Cullompton: Willan. This text, authored by academics with practitioner experience, provides a valuable reference point throughout policing studies.

O'Neill, M (2018) *Key Challenges in Criminal Investigation*. Bristol: Policy Press. This book brings a critical viewpoint to the investigative environment.

CHAPTER 2
KEY PRINCIPLES OF CRIMINAL INVESTIGATION

LEARNING OBJECTIVES

AFTER READING THIS CHAPTER YOU WILL BE ABLE TO:

- interpret the golden hour principles;
- demonstrate an investigative mindset;
- explain material attrition factors;
- categorise stages of investigation.

INTRODUCTION

Section 22 of the Criminal Procedure and Investigations Act (CPIA) 1996 defines a criminal investigation as

> *An investigation conducted by police officers with a view to it being ascertained*
>
> a) *Whether a person should be charged with an offence, or*
>
> b) *Whether a person charged with an offence is guilty of it.*

Innes (2003) declares a criminal investigation to be a form of information work, concerned with the identification, interpretation and ordering of information with the objective of ascertaining whether a crime has occurred and, if so, who was involved and how. The Core Investigative Doctrine (ACPO, 2012a) starts by suggesting that an investigation is an effective search for material to bring an offender to justice.

Often likened to a jigsaw puzzle, criminal investigation requires a comprehensive picture to be assembled. In a jigsaw, the pieces are already available; the skill is in the assembly. Imagine if the parts were spread over a variety of locations and then add the proposal that you must identify the location before you can search for the piece. Sometimes people will help; other times they will hinder, either purposefully or accidentally. Some pieces present themselves, while others are hidden. This everyday depiction of an investigation would challenge the most experienced puzzler.

In contrast to the jigsaw, not all the material you gather will be relevant or reliable. Not all lines of investigation will be fruitful. This chapter will recommend approaches to complement your investigations, examining influences, bias and preconceptions which influence your decision making before moving on to established principles on which to base your initial investigation.

INVESTIGATIVE MINDSET

The Core Investigative Doctrine (ACPO, 2012a) introduced the concept of an investigative mindset. This model is designed to complement an understanding of bias and the working rules which affect your decision making. The investigative mindset consists of five principles.

1. UNDERSTANDING THE SOURCE OF THE MATERIAL

Having an appreciation of where the material originated, its provenance and characteristics will assist the analysis. When considering a witness, ask yourself: do they have connections with the incident? Are other people involved? Are they vulnerable? Can they have witnessed what they claim? All of the above will contribute to their credibility and the importance or otherwise of their testimony.

Closed-circuit television (CCTV) predominates both public and private areas and is important for most investigations. Where is the camera located; what is the operating system; are there any blind spots? Is the time print accurate? These are all questions a competent investigator should consider.

2. PLANNING AND PREPARATION

You now have the material. What are your objectives for examining it? What is the best way to perform the examination? Do you need any specialist equipment? Where will you conduct the examination?

Going back to the example of the witness above, you might ask yourself the following questions: How will you interview the witness? Do they have any specialist requirements? How will you record the interview? Where is the best place to conduct it?

In the case of CCTV: What are you looking for? How will you view it? Is any equipment required? How will you preserve the recording?

3. EXAMINATION

This can be sub-divided into three phases: account, clarification and challenge.

Consider what is known and unknown. Can you identify consistencies or contradictions? If so, how will you clarify them? This can be summarised as the A, B, C approach (Stelfox, 2012).

- **A**ssume nothing.

- **B**elieve nothing.

- **C**hallenge everything.

The most used reflective question an investigator can ever pose is: Why?

4. RECORDING AND COLLATION

The ultimate assessment of any investigation is in court. An effective pass mark of 100 per cent represents the criminal burden of proof that requires a prosecution to prove all elements of the offence beyond all reasonable doubt. It is worth suggesting that if it is not recorded or written down, a court will question it. Workloads and passage of time mean it is unlikely you will remember all salient points. Record how you obtained, stored and examined the material. Your findings should all be recorded in the most appropriate manner.

5. EVALUATION

Collecting and examining material will not assist an investigation in isolation. What have you discovered; does this open new or close existing lines of enquiry? The Criminal Procedure and Investigations Act places a duty on investigators to follow all reasonable lines of enquiry, whether they point towards or away from identified suspects. The investigator should identify any actions to further enquiries in the evaluation stage.

Newburn et al's (2007) authoritative text stresses that applying the investigative mindset encourages investigators to maintain an open-minded approach, remaining receptive to alternative views or explanations. This is an essential investigative trait.

The next example of investigative practice has the potential to touch all aspects of your investigation. You are already an experienced decision maker: from crossing a road to career choices, your analysis and selection of options demonstrates your decision making. Studying the practice of decision making highlights traits which can be incorporated into your decision making.

BIAS

The dangers of bias, stereotyping and perceptions on your practice can be minimised by applying the investigative mindset. Recognising that such influences can affect investigative choices merits some explanation about commonly encountered examples.

Heuristics are cognitive 'shortcuts' which we all use to simplify decision making. The relevance to investigative practice is emphasised by Tversky and Kahneman's (1974) suggestion that heuristics are most likely to be deployed in periods of uncertainty. Dynamic situations such as investigations, where practitioners arrive at conclusions quickly, tend to depend on heuristics rather than facts. Heuristics can be linked to Simon's (1956) study, which coined the notion of 'satisficing' where the decision maker seeks the first workable option rather than the best one.

References to bias are predominantly negative; for example, racist or sexist approaches are recognised as undesirable. More subtle personal biases encountered include:

- belief bias, where personal beliefs predominate;

- attentional bias, neglecting important matters which occur after less important aspects;

- disposition effect, where the information possessed outweighs that which has been sought;

- capability bias, commonly encountered in target-driven philosophies;

- authority bias, deferring to those with presumed seniority or expertise.

The above will result in decisions being reached on a subjective basis rather than the desired objective basis of the National Decision Model (Chapter 3).

The truly experienced investigator acknowledges the value of experience but does not allow it to dominate. Investigators require precision, which is unlikely to be found in broad, base rate fallacies. For example, needing a coat when visiting the Lake District may be sound advice, but is it statistically reliable?

EVIDENCE-BASED POLICING

On 31 January 2000, the investigation into the activities of Harold Shipman culminated in his conviction for the murder of 15 people. The second report of the Shipman Enquiry, chaired by Dame Janet Smith DBE (2003), examined the conduct of an earlier (1998) investigation based on concerns about Shipman's practice, which had concluded they were unfounded. Smith's report was critical of the investigative ability of the officers, concluding that the senior investigating officer was *'out of his depth'* (Smith, 2003, p 133). Analysis of the circumstances suggest that personal heuristics and influences such as authority bias influenced the depth to which some lines of enquiry were pursued, resulting in inadequate material being obtained. The circumstances led to the development and publication of *An SIO's Guide to Investigating Unexpected Death and Serious Harm in Healthcare Settings* (NPCC, 2015), confirming the benefits of reflection to guide future procedure.

INITIAL STAGES

Criminal investigation can be sub-divided into reactive and proactive elements. The traditional view of the public is that of the reactive investigator, responding to an event. Proactive investigations are normally intelligence based, focused on forecasted events which are yet to occur. Both types of enquiry amount to criminal investigations.

Criminal Procedure and Investigations Act (CPIA) codes of practice (2015) recognise the variety of investigative initiations, explaining that an investigation includes:

1. investigations into crimes that have been committed;

2. investigations whose purpose is to ascertain whether a crime has been committed, with a view to the possible institution of criminal proceedings;

3. investigations which begin in the belief that a crime may be committed, with a view to the possible institution of criminal proceedings.

CPIA requirements are a vital component of all prosecutions and are discussed further in Chapter 9.

The early stages of an investigation are when material is at its most abundant and available. During these primary stages, the focus is wide, concentrating on collecting the maximum amount of information possible, guided by the golden hour principles which will be described later in this chapter. As the investigation progresses and lines of enquiry are identified, your lens will focus. To use a shopping analogy, when you make your way into a large shop your focus is wide; as you identify items you would like to buy, you concentrate on those articles, bringing a more precise focus to your search, resulting in your selection of one item. Similarly with an investigation, you move from a mass trawl for material to specific enquiries. The initial stages represent a low-focus, large-amount gathering of material. The 5WH approach proposed by Stelfox (2012) is useful at this stage, where you ask:

- who – key individual(s);
- what – activities;
- where – geographical scope;
- when – time frame;
- why – motive;
- how – method of operation.

Structuring your initial questioning using the above approach is helpful in providing a fundamental base to your enquiries

GOLDEN HOUR PRINCIPLES

The importance of a structured approach in the initial stages of an investigation is represented by the golden hour principles. First introduced in the Core Investigative Doctrine (ACPO, 2012a), they continue to feature in practice advice through the College of Policing Authorised Professional Practice (College of Policing, 2021c) web pages.

Do not be misled by the term 'hour'; these principles apply throughout the initial stages of an investigation when material is most abundant. The following ten elements will now be explored individually:

- victims;
- scenes;

- suspects;
- witnesses;
- log;
- family/community;
- physical evidence;
- intelligence;
- prevent contamination;
- lines of responsibility.

VICTIMS

The initial stages of many investigations are chaotic; it is not always apparent who the victims are. It is vital that they are recognised at the earliest opportunity; most importantly, remember that medical attention always takes precedence over investigative requirements. In many cases, your victim represents a specific crime scene and, as such, a wealth of material from forensic to verbal accounts is available. Sensitivity is paramount; you may be used to the restrictions of crime scene management, but the victim, their friends and family will prioritise support over any contamination issues. Your role is often to explain in ordinary terms what you are trying to achieve. As with any crime scene, try to preserve a victim as appropriately as possible. A simple 'what happened?' may provide information to help at this early stage. Take note of the suggestions in Chapter 5 regarding maximising material gained through questioning. Investigative actions are often based on these initial accounts: confirm credibility and veracity where you can.

SCENES

A criminal event can generate a variety of crime scenes. The location, victims, offenders, witnesses, transport and deposition sites all represent crime scenes. Initial attenders should endeavour to preserve them to provide the best opportunity of harvesting useful material. Controlling access to locations and preventing contamination creates an environment to give any future forensic results reliability. Locard's exchange principle (1923) confirms that 'every contact leaves a trace'. When you walk into a crime scene, you carry material from elsewhere on your shoes, clothes and anything else, which is then introduced into that scene. This is why you see forensic officers wearing sterile clothing to avoid this. You should think about this whenever you attend a crime scene.

POLICING SPOTLIGHT

Cordoning crime scenes tends to attract members of the public. The vast majority will not interfere with the cordon or scene. Occasionally, however, you may encounter someone who is not persuaded and remains intent on following a route through the crime scene. Such an occasion led to the stated case of *DPP v Morrison* [2003]. A crime scene had been established in a shopping centre. Morrison attempted to walk through the cordoned area and was stopped by an officer. Morrison was not dissuaded and continued his journey, where he was arrested for police obstruction under the terms of the Police Act 1996 and section 5 of the Public Order Act 1986. The matter was heard in a magistrates' court and Morrison was convicted. The conviction was appealed on the grounds that the officer was not 'in the execution of his duty' at the time of the offence and had no power or authority to prevent him continuing his journey. The appeal was successful. The legal position of maintaining crime scenes is of such importance that a further appeal was allowed, which resulted in the following findings.

- There is no statutory power for a police cordon to close off a public area. The only specific authority is found in section 33 of the Terrorism Act 2000.

- Referring to the earlier case of *Ghani v Jones* [1970], the police should be able to do whatever is necessary and reasonable to preserve evidence of a crime.

Providing actions are necessary and proportionate, officers can restrict access to a crime scene even though there is no statutory power to do so. If you are called upon to explain your position in restricting access to a crime scene, the Morrison findings will support your actions.

Crime scenes tell a variety of stories that you as an investigator can interpret, in addition to preserving a scene for forensic examination; examples include the following.

- Is there CCTV coverage?

- What is the telecommunications coverage like?

- Which communications mast does coverage originate from?

- Is the scene overlooked?

- What are the potential arrival and exit routes?

- Would the event have created noise? If so, who may have heard it?

These are just a few examples. To borrow from the world of fictional detectives, do the circumstances suggest something should be present which is not? In *The Adventure of Silver Blaze*, Sherlock Holmes investigated the theft of a racehorse and murder of the trainer. Linking the stable crime scene to the discovery that the stable dog had not barked during the crime led to the hypothesis that the offender was a regular visitor, explaining that the '*curious incident of the dog in the night-time is that the dog made no noise because no stranger was present*' (Conan Doyle, 1892, p 9).

SUSPECTS

All the discussion at the start of this chapter about what constitutes a criminal investigation refers to tracing an offender. The decision to refer to someone as a suspect has a number of ramifications throughout the Police and Criminal Evidence Act 1984 (PACE), such as cautioning and identification rules. Suspicion must be genuine, proportionate, reasonable and objective. Often based on information, intelligence, behaviours or questioning, suspicion has a lower threshold than belief. On a scale of 1–10, suspicion will be at the lower end with belief at the upper end. Figure 2.1 depicts this sliding scale.

		SUSPICION					BELIEF			
1	2	3	4	5	6	7	8	9	10	

Figure 2.1 Suspicion–belief scale

Innes (2002) refers to 'self-solving' and 'whodunnit' investigations. Suspects are identified in the initial response in a self-solver, while whodunnits are more complex in nature. Although Innes' research was based on murder investigations, parallels can be drawn with volume crime investigations. The early response is vital in both instances. CPIA codes of practice instruct investigators to follow all reasonable lines of enquiry, whether these point towards or away from the suspect, ensuring the whole matter is investigated rather than simply building a case against an identified suspect.

A suspect represents a potential crime scene; it is important to guard against physical contamination and that of their account by acquaintances or co-suspects. Refer to Chapter 5 for guidance on unsolicited comments made by suspects.

WITNESSES

Witnesses present an exceptional source of information. A witness may have memories based on what they have seen, heard, touched, tasted or smelled. They will have views and opinions, representing a source of intelligence about the area and those involved. In short, they are an all-round information source. As with self-solving investigations, witnesses are often found at the scene of the offence. You must differentiate between onlookers and witnesses, and should take action to trace those witnesses present as soon as possible. It is acceptable to obtain a first account and arrange interviews at mutually convenient times. Chapter 5 discusses the PEACE interview model and questioning styles, both of which should be considered when obtaining witness accounts. Chapter 4 explores witness and victim management.

LOG

The log element refers to the recording of decisions and actions. This represents your record and should include conditions, circumstances and resources. You will have to refer to your log in the future, as the influences on your decisions may have been forgotten. Decisions should always be accompanied by your rationale. Occasionally, decisions will contradict normal practice; the log enables you to justify actions taken and those not proceeded with. It is important to record what you first encountered, scene parameters, details of who was afforded access and directions given throughout the initial period. All are useful and should be recorded in sufficient detail to recall the decision, influences and rationale. Dando and Ormerod (2017) found the recording of decisions assisted practitioners in overcoming bias in their decision making. CPIA reinforces the requirement to record, retain and reveal details of your investigation. A well-drafted log will be a valuable asset to your investigation and any subsequent prosecution.

Scene management is complemented by comprehensive log-keeping, including any observations made. When, how and where was a cordon created? Who has been authorised to breach the parameters, and why?

FAMILIES AND COMMUNITY

The potential impact of criminal behaviours on families and communities is famously explained in Wilson and Kelling's (1982) 'broken windows' article. The golden hour principles reflect supportive actions that can be applied at the start of an investigation, shaping a situation to avoid long-term effects. In the public arena, information voids require filling; the drama of crime and criminal behaviour attracts attention and discussion. In the era of 24-hour news and social media, these voids can be filled in many ways, both helpful and unhelpful. Ensuring those most affected are provided with accurate and timely information is vital in maintaining confidence and trust between families, communities and investigators. This engagement facilitates investigators' understanding of needs, concerns and expectations, which should be incorporated into their communications. It is important to avoid promises or supposition, and to maintain a professional demeanour. Many crimes have a sensitive element; you should recognise that different people have different sensitivities, and show empathy in your duties.

Traditional and social media represent useful opportunities to convey messages or appeals to the widest possible audience (see the discussion of media strategy in Chapter 3). However, you should always seek advice from your press office before utilising this method of appeal.

PHYSICAL EVIDENCE

The golden hour principles refer to preservation of evidence. In the initial stages, you should concentrate on accumulating as much relevant material as possible, as evidential admissibility can be assessed as the investigation progresses. For example, a witness who tells you they overheard a conversation is providing valuable information, although the hearsay element may preclude this from becoming evidence. Your investigation would use the information, and the information may become evidence through these enquiries. Legislation such as the General Data Protection Regulations (GDPR) dictates retention periods. The practical capacity of storage affects how long material such as CCTV recordings are retained. A large organisation will retain material in accordance with the Data Protection Act 2018, while an independent shopkeeper will have a limited storage capacity before coverage is 'recorded over'. This can vary from several days to a more limited period. Devices such as dash cams are dependent on the storage capacity of memory cards, which commonly overwrite data every 20 to 120 minutes. You must be aware of your powers to seize material.

Section 1 of PACE can be briefly summarised as follows: that the power is based on reasonable grounds to suspect (see Figure 2.1) that stolen, prohibited or sharply pointed or

KEY PRINCIPLES OF CRIMINAL INVESTIGATION

bladed articles may be found, then an officer may detain and search any person, vehicle or anything in that vehicle. The power may be exercised in any place to which the public have access at the time.

Section 19 of PACE provides a general power to seize property when a police officer is lawfully on the premises, providing the officer has reasonable grounds to believe (see Figure 2.1) that if the items were not seized, they would be liable to be concealed, lost, altered, damaged or destroyed. The mnemonic CLAD is helpful in remembering this element.

- **C**oncealed

- **L**ost

- **A**ltered

- **D**amaged or destroyed

Please note that this power does not apply to public places.

Section 22 of PACE allows lawfully seized property to be retained for as long as necessary, for use as evidence at a trial for forensic examination or other investigation in connection with an offence. It is worthy of note that section 22(4) states that *'nothing may be retained... if a photograph or copy would be sufficient...'*

Acknowledging the expansion of digitally stored material, section 20 of PACE allows an officer lawfully on the premises to request information stored on a computer to be produced in a visible, legible format which can be taken away. The theme of recognising mass storage challenges is continued with the Criminal Justice and Police Act 2001 Part 2, which provides the power known as seize and sift. This legislates for the situation where a preliminary analysis suggests it is not practical to examine the material in situ. The material may be seized for examination elsewhere, provided the officers' presence is lawful and they have a legal power of seizure.

Search powers such as sections 18 and 32 of PACE, which are dependent upon arrest, are discussed elsewhere in this series.

REFLECTIVE PRACTICE 2.1

LEVEL 6

The dangers of poor management of crime scenes can be illustrated through the case *R v Hoey* [2007], which sent shockwaves through the investigative and scientific community when the use of low copy number DNA was suspended by the Crown Prosecution Service. The trial judge, Mr Justice Weir, summarised the approach as thoughtless and slapdash: there was a lack of protective clothing and a lack of proof as to who had done what, creating a situation where items were widely and routinely handled with disregard for their integrity; he concluded that DNA evidence should not be allowed in the trial. The situation triggered *A Review of the Science of Low Template DNA Analysis* (Caddy et al, 2008), which concluded the technique was sound, providing actions surrounding the collection and preservation of samples were addressed correctly.

Can you estimate the impact on investigations of being unable to use DNA science? Evaluate the impact of this on:

a) the public;

b) criminals.

INTELLIGENCE

Intelligence is frequently associated with secrecy, and some intelligence does require secrecy as well as elements of confidentiality. However, this does not represent most intelligence. You already have an internal intelligence database you use in daily life, such as social venues you like to use and others you would rather avoid, transport routes and favourite foods. Recognising that you represent an intelligence source leads to the realisation that everyone else is also a potential source of information.

The benefits of accessing locally based intelligence based on people's observations, thoughts and experiences feature in Innes' (2006) study, demonstrating the importance of community intelligence in a counter-terrorism environment. The insight 'you cannot recognise abnormal behaviours if you do not know what is normal' places the adage of 'knowing your patch' firmly within contemporary policing.

The National Intelligence Model (NIM) is a core feature of policing activity. The nature of this model means it generates intelligence. A large amount of intelligence is already held ready to be accessed, providing you with a base to interrogate.

Professionally held databases will provide you with:

- community intelligence;

- crime patterns;

- modus operandi (MO) analysis;

- nominal information.

Discussions with members of the public, witnesses, house-to-house enquiries and community groups will all provide information which, while not evidential, will be useful in guiding your enquiries.

Intelligence specialists will assist your enquiries, while analysts, covert human intelligence source (CHIS) departments and community officers are resources you are encouraged to engage with.

Social media represents one element of what is known as open-source material. Open forum discussions often present valuable intelligence and may be viewed as assisting information gathering. You should seek advice from your intelligence specialists about using this valuable source of information.

PREVENTING CONTAMINATION

The dangers of contamination are present in each element of the golden hour principles. Victims' memories can be affected by exposure to alternative accounts or media coverage. Loftus and Palmer's classic 1974 experiment highlights how questioning techniques have the potential to influence answers, in effect creating false memories. The victim's status as a crime scene can be corrupted by the same factors impacting any scene. Your emotional intelligence is likely to be tested in preserving a traumatised victim to maximise the forensic value. Each situation must be judged on its own merits; explaining your reasoning in a calm and measured manner is likely to instil confidence and understanding. It is good practice to refer to victims by their name rather than the term victim, complainant or injured party. Humanising creates a positive environment.

An arrest strategy is a feature of long-term enquiries. The nature of golden hour decision making is often dynamic (see Chapter 3 for further examination of decisions and strategy). The identification and arrest of suspects will be more dynamic when occurring in this initial period. Make sure your professional knowledge regarding arrest, search and allied matters such as significant statements (Chapter 5) supports this dynamic environment. Your actions and interactions will be subject to legal analysis. Professional decision making aligned to the National Decision Model (see Chapter 3) is imperative. Suspects as crime scenes are subject to similar contamination as are victims, and your actions must be designed to minimise this.

Witnesses may be discovered in the golden hour phase or as a result of enquiries originating in this period. You may have to prioritise obtaining statements now rather than doing this at a later time. In all cases, avoid leading questions and obtain first accounts. The progress of the enquiry and safety issues are dependent upon you obtaining the maximum amount of information as quickly as possible. You will not be able to exclude exposure to information which may influence memories; you can, however, discover how much, if any, influence this has had on the witness during your questioning. As with any material, you must take steps to confirm its credibility. Your role as an investigator includes assessing the provenance and credibility of all material.

Discussions about crime scenes are regularly accompanied by pictures of crime scene tape, illustrating the importance of establishing and maintaining a sterile area. This approach extends to people and vehicles, which are regularly crime scenes themselves. Decide on your scene parameters in an objective way. It is always possible to make your scene smaller as the information picture emerges. Extending a scene into areas which have already been contaminated is feasible but should be avoided through your original decision making. Ensure your practical approach to seizing material is well informed and appropriate. Do not unnecessarily interfere with a crime scene: simply opening a window has the potential to alter an internal scene. External scenes are subject to the vagaries of the weather; coverings such as scene tents or stepping boards are ideal but subject to delay in arriving at a scene. Use anything which may be to hand to provide some protection when recording your actions and reasoning. Ensure your contacts with victims, witnesses and suspects take contamination concerns into account to minimise their effect.

POLICING SPOTLIGHT

The case of *Swinney v Chief Constable of Northumbria Police Force* [1997] illustrates the dangers of poor practice. Mr and Mrs Swinney provided information to the police regarding the offenders in a serious investigation; the information was recorded and then left in an unattended police vehicle from which it was subsequently stolen. The information was passed to the offenders with foreseeable results. The case refers to a claim of negligence against the police on behalf of the sources of the information. As with many investigative decisions, a lack of care cannot only jeopardise future actions; the consequences for investigators, the public and community can be significant. These can be addressed simply through a considered, professional approach. Hindsight will challenge your approach, and should be used as a reflective opportunity to inform your future practice.

LINES OF RESPONSIBILITY

Golden hour principles refer to identifying, informing, briefing, co-ordinating and reviewing. As the responding officer, you will be responsible for all these elements on your arrival. Victims, witnesses and members of the public will see an officer arriving to take control; they will not be aware of your specialisms or experience – at that point you represent the police. This is where your leadership skills come to the fore, assessing the situation, directing people and taking action. Consider leadership as an approach to your attendance. As you are at the beginning of your career, you may see supervisory colleagues or rank as a mark of leadership. Distance yourself from this view for a moment. How do the actors involved in the crime see you at this point? You have arrived on the scene as a leader.

Ensure you have all the available information to guide your golden hour decisions. History of the location, methods, victims or offenders will be available to attending officers through intelligence databases. It is important that members of the public view you as professional; demonstrating awareness is the first step towards this. Analyse the situation from your own observations and the information you glean from others at the scene. Borrowing from questioning styles, 'Tell me?' provides an ideal starting question (see Chapter 5). If you think colleagues or specialists are required, make that request along with an update on your initial findings. If colleagues are present, someone needs to co-ordinate the response. If the situation has generated a multi-agency response, it is imperative that this is managed. Effective briefing is vital. The IIMARCH model favoured by the College of Policing (2020) provides a framework for briefings appropriate to all situations.

- **I**nformation: When did it happen; what has happened; where did it happen; how did it happen; who is involved; what has happened since; what have you done?

- **I**ntention: What have you achieved; what is the aim?

- **M**ethod: How will you achieve these aims; are any specialists requested?

- **A**dministration: Further requirements; details of log; identified issues; public, media, local requirements.

- **R**isk assessment: Identified weaknesses and threats; measures taken or required.

- **C**ommunications: Ensure all relevant parties are aware of the current situation; this can expand to refer to the public and media.

- **H**umanitarian issues: Identified rights issues.

This framework cultivates an accurate, unambiguous briefing delivered with appropriate brevity.

Reviewing is an important element of all investigations; as more information is acquired, earlier decisions may no longer be appropriate. Updating your decisions is a sign of professionalism, while failing to acknowledge a changing environment is not.

The golden hour principles apply to both self-solvers and whodunnit investigations, providing a framework for a complete investigation and a fundamentally solid foundation for longer enquiries.

CRITICAL THINKING ACTIVITY 2.1

LEVEL 6

The golden hour principles originated in 2005 and were updated in 2012. Technological and digital environments have developed rapidly since this time. Evaluate the principles to ascertain if they continue to represent best practice in contemporary society.

The golden hour principles represent the initial stages of an investigation, as outlined in the Core Investigative Doctrine (ACPO, 2012a). It is important to now introduce a metaphorical pause, to evaluate the material. An understanding of the rules of evidence (see Chapter 3) is helpful in the evaluation stage. Evaluations are organic in nature; they are represented as a pause here, but should be consistently applied throughout the enquiry. If the material identifies a suspect, you will then proceed to suspect management. Where this does not occur, you will enter the further investigation phase, cycling between that and evaluation until no further actions are available or a suspect is identified (suspect management will also be explored in Chapter 3). The suspect management phase is followed by a return to evidential evaluation. If the material is deemed sufficient to support a prosecution, the charging phase followed by case management and court follow. If the material is insufficient to support a charge, cycles of further investigation and evaluation are repeated before moving to charge or no charge.

POLICING SPOTLIGHT

On 2 June 2010, Derrick Bird shot and killed 12 people, injuring a further 11 in the area of Whitehaven, Cumbria. The shootings ended with Bird committing suicide a short distance away. Enquiries confirmed him to be a lone gunman; there was no suggestion any other person was involved in the preparation or acts. This major investigation continued by examining the circumstances leading up to and the events themselves, on behalf of the coroner. The enquiry followed the lines of any criminal investigation, even though no criminal trial would take place. You may become involved in investigations where no one will be prosecuted. Such investigations identify matters to inform future practice as well as identifying hitherto unknown accomplices or conspirators. It is important that where circumstances prevent prosecutions, the enquiry is conducted to identical professional standards.

CONCLUSION

Criminal investigations are varied and complex, and generic approaches provide no basis to a successful enquiry. Common themes condensed from reflections on practice present viable investigative guidance. This chapter has outlined steps to support both lengthy and brief investigations through a comprehensive approach from the earliest stages. Influences on decision making have been presented to aid the identification and selection of feasible alternatives in decision making. Legislative requirements are aligned to the investigative process. The chapter culminated in an explanation of which investigative phases follow, taking your investigation from instigation to conclusion.

SUMMARY OF KEY CONCEPTS

This chapter has introduced you to the investigative process. The content equips you to:

- recognise when an investigation starts;

- identify influences on decision making;

- interpret the golden hour principles to create appropriate investigative actions;

- align legislative requirements with the investigative process.

This prepares you to conduct criminal investigations from instigation to conclusion.

CHECK YOUR KNOWLEDGE

1. You receive information that a group of criminals are recruiting people to supply controlled drugs in your local town. A proactive investigation is mounted to enquire into this. You identify a time and location when the organised crime group intend to meet an identified dealer and supply them with controlled drugs. You arrange covert observations with a view to arresting any persons identified as being involved in criminality. This results in a number of people being arrested. At what stage does your investigation begin?

    a) when drugs are seen to change hands;

    b) at the point of arrest;

    c) when observations are authorised;

    d) when information is received.

2. The phrase 'every contact leaves a trace' is attributable to which principle?

3. Which powers allow you to seize and retain property when lawfully on the premises?

4. Outline the elements of the IIMARCH briefing model.

Sample answers to these questions are provided at the end of the book.

FURTHER READING

The College of Policing Authorised Professional Practice (APP) web pages provide a searchable resource, covering many aspects of policing including investigative interviewing. The guidance can be found at: www.app.college.police.uk

Tong, S, Bryant, R and Horvath, M (2009) *Understanding Criminal Investigation*. Malden, MA: Wiley.
This text relates theory to practice and is written by authors with experience of the nexus between policing and academia.

CHAPTER 3
INVESTIGATIVE PRACTICE

LEARNING OBJECTIVES

AFTER READING THIS CHAPTER YOU WILL BE ABLE TO:

- **demonstrate comprehensive decision making;**

- **evaluate investigative information;**

- **formulate investigative strategies;**

- **interpret material to develop investigative hypothesis.**

INTRODUCTION

As your investigation progresses, the high-yield, low-focus approach of the instigation phase becomes more focused as you identify lines of enquiry. Innes (2003) describes investigation as a form of information work where interpretation of the material equips you to draw inferences and develop a hypothesis. This requires you to not only seek material but to then evaluate it. Information evaluation creates a hierarchy of material where value and relevance vary. You will make judgements as to which material you then base further enquiries on. This chapter will equip you to address the initial stages of an investigation, explaining how material availability is affected by attrition. You are encouraged to recognise this attrition rate by employing the golden hour principles, exploring how to professionalise your decision making before evaluating your findings.

MATERIAL ATTRITION

All events generate material. Victims' and offenders' actions, eyewitnesses' accounts, biological material, digital data and passive data generators represent valuable sources of information to populate your investigative picture. As time passes, the value of this material can deteriorate. Individual memories fade and become contaminated. Biological material can be affected by weather conditions or deliberate attempts to taint it. Data can become corrupted. A series of attritional factors will decrease the amount of all available material in a chronological fashion. This rate of attrition is depicted in Figure 3.1, which illustrates that the amount of material generated cannot all be gathered, nor will all the material acquired meet the rules of evidence. Hence the prosecution will be supported by a fraction of the material generated by the event. Material gathered which does not meet admissibility criteria will be classed as unused, which is something that will be explored further in Chapter 9. The investigative aim is to minimise the erosion of material.

Chapter 2 explained what a criminal investigation is; the code of practice to the Criminal Procedure and Investigations Act 1996 explains that an investigation starts when:

1. a crime has been committed; or

2. an investigation whose purpose is to ascertain whether a crime has been committed; or

3. investigations which begin in the belief that a crime may be committed.

Figure 3.1 Material attrition funnel

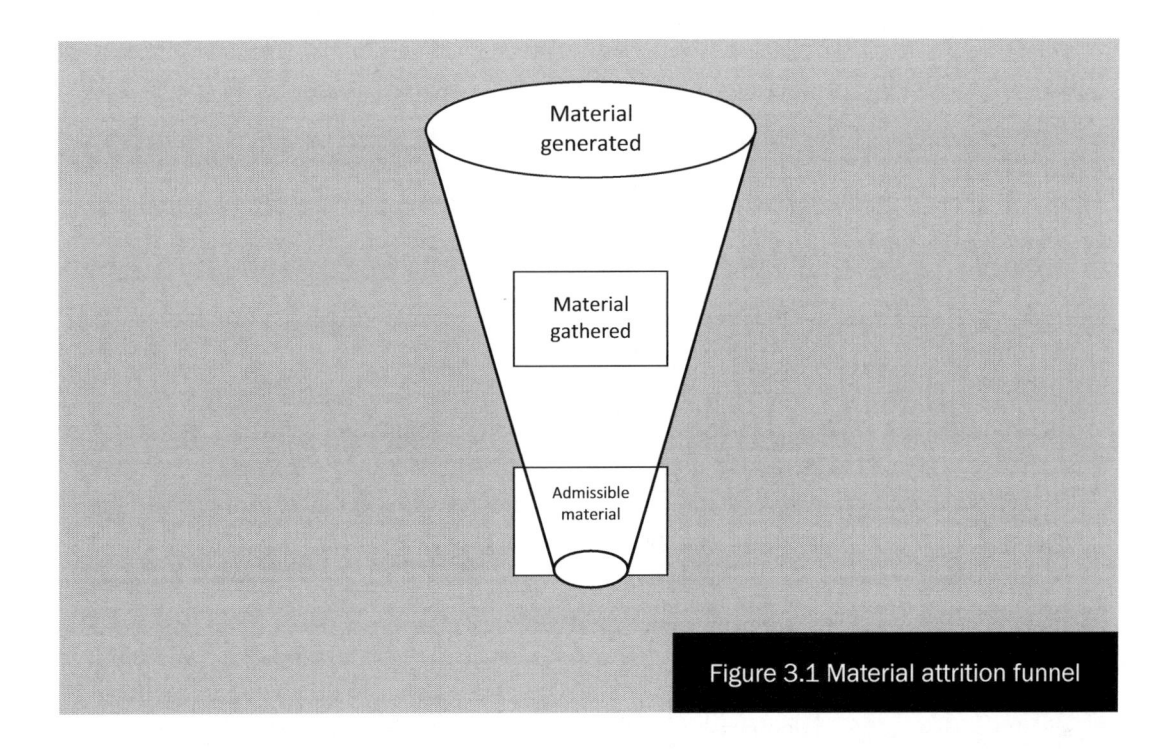

Examples may include:

1. you receive a report of a crime having occurred from a victim or witness;

2. you stop and search a person carrying items you believe may be stolen;

3. you maintain observations following intelligence that an offence is due to take place.

In each case, the start of your actions signifies the start of the investigation. As explained in the previous chapter, this includes a requirement to pursue all reasonable lines of enquiry and record, retain and subsequently reveal all relevant material (detailed in Chapter 9). This recording of material extends to your decision making, which is summarised next.

DECISION MAKING

Decision making involves gathering and interpreting facts and evaluating their impact in a relevant ethical context. This process often produces moral dilemmas (Tong et al, 2009). Philippa Foot's 1967 ethical 'trolleyology' experiment, where participants are asked to choose between doing nothing, which is likely to result in serious harm, or reacting in a way that is likely to cause serious harm to a smaller number of people, illustrates the challenges of decision making in highly charged situations.

According to Cole (2004, p 214), decision making is *'a process of identifying a problem, evaluating alternatives, and selecting one alternative'*. This is something you practise individually and in groups many times a day. From crossing the road to deciding what to eat, you are an accomplished decision maker. There are two key types of decision making which we will explore further: traditional and naturalistic.

Traditional decision making assumes complete certainty of information and options, as well as time to analyse and arrive at a decision. Bounded rationality in decision making can be linked to bias, as described in Chapter 2; this is where the decision maker arrives at a decision that will do rather than pursuing the optimal decision, a practice known as satisficing (Simon, 1990).

Naturalistic decision making involves fast, complex decision making by experts in time-pressured situations. This type of decision making arises from research into the mistaken shooting down of the Iranian passenger plane by the USS Vincennes in 1988. In this tragic event, experts in a time-critical situation wrongly identified a threat, taking steps to negate that threat and then developing a rapid hypothesis and balancing risk, resulting in a significantly flawed decision; this shows the limitations of human analysis in stressful situations. Naturalistic decision making concentrates on cognitive functions, situational awareness, making sense of situations and planning, emphasising the importance of knowledge and experience.

INVESTIGATIVE DECISION MAKING

Making and taking decisions is a vital part of investigative work. Innes (2007, p 271) describes five decision types you will encounter in major crime investigations.

1. Policy decisions. Taken by the investigator, setting parameters for the investigation. Commonly referred to as 'strategies'.

2. Knowledge decisions. How information should be interpreted and analysed.

3. Action decisions. What should be done, when, by whom. Prioritising areas of investigation.

4. Logistic decisions. Infrastructure, staffing.

5. Legal decisions: Does your decision require legislative support in terms of law or powers to act?

Professions such as medicine recognise that decisions have the potential to lead to harm. Investigative decision making has historically avoided situations where negligence would lead to legal remedy being sought. *Hill v CC West Yorkshire Police* [1989] provided a shield for allegations of negligence in investigations, claiming that this was in the public interest, a situation the case of *Commissioner of Police of the Metropolis (Appellant) v DSD and another (Respondents)* [2018] UKSC 11 on appeal from [2015] EWCA Civ 646, addressed. The case, which was brought by two victims of convicted rapist John Worboys, centred on elements of the investigation which had proven negligent. While Hill prevented a negligence claim against the police, Article 3 of the Human Rights Act 1998 provides that all citizens should be protected from inhuman or degrading treatment, a situation the Supreme Court found had not occurred in this case. In effect, where negligence in investigations results in further harms, the police may be liable for their actions.

As one of the most regularly practised human calculations, decision making has been subject to much study. Policing in England and Wales adopted the National Decision Model (NDM) in 2011. This replaced a variety of models linked to an assortment of situations to simplify matters, so that officers become experienced in one form of decision making and the associated rationale. The National Decision Model reflects eight elements of traditional decision making where:

1. problems are recognised and defined;

2. information is gathered;

3. alternative actions are identified;

4. evaluation criteria is introduced;

5. alternative routes are evaluated;

6. an optimal alternative is chosen;

7. the agreed solution is implemented;

8. the agreed solution is evaluated.

CRIMINAL INVESTIGATION

The NDM condenses this into a five-stage cyclical model as interpreted in Figure 3.2.

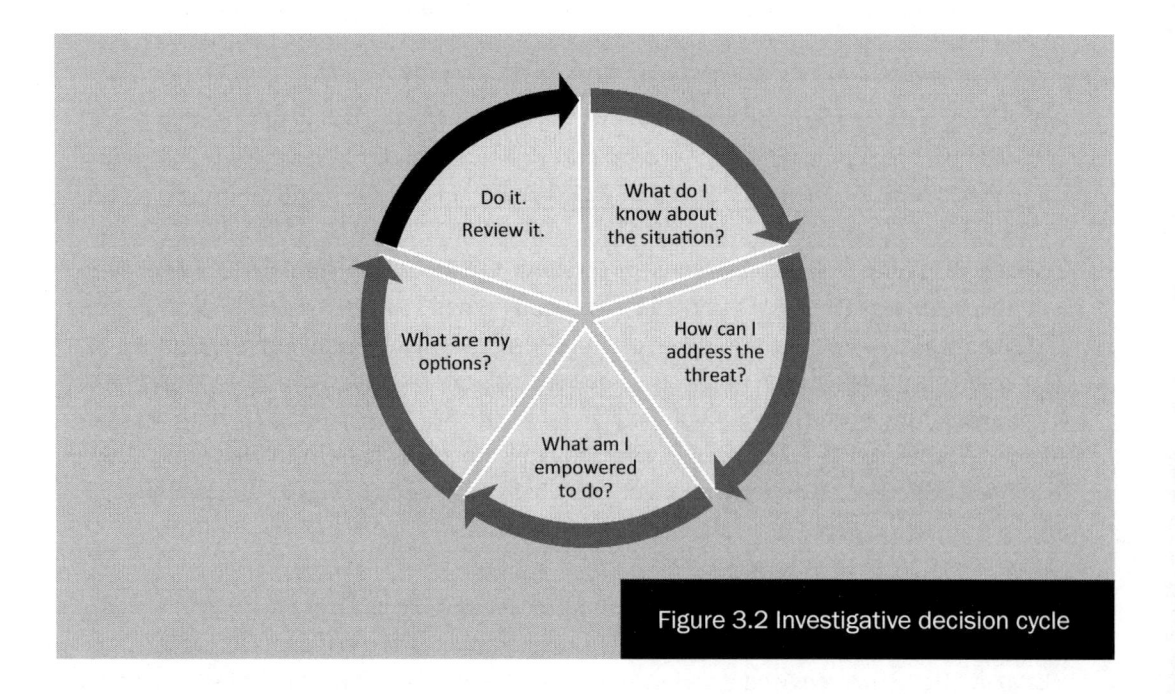

Figure 3.2 Investigative decision cycle

Centred on the police code of ethics, the NDM starts with the following criteria.

1. Gathering of information or intelligence.

2. Assessing the threat and developing a working strategy.

3. Decision makers must then consider applicable powers and policy before identifying.

4. Options and contingencies.

5. The identified action then takes place with a review of the ensuing situation and result.

The College of Policing (2013a) recommend the mnemonic CIAPOAR to help remember the elements of the model.

- **C**ode of Ethics

- **I**nformation

- **A**ssessment

- **P**owers and policy

- **O**ptions

- **A**ction

- **R**eview

This model is particularly suitable across the limitless boundaries of policing and officers' experience. Senior investigating officers in serious or organised investigative environments, which are often complex and dynamic in nature and where decisions will have consequences or ramifications, bring their expertise and experience to complement the model in a more naturalistic style.

Each criminal investigation will require a myriad of decisions. Timescales between events and court examinations are lengthening all the time: months if not years are becoming increasingly common. You will not be able to remember all the influences from the time; therefore, recording your decision making is imperative. The NDM provides an ideal template for this recording.

REFLECTIVE PRACTICE 3.1

LEVEL 4

Consider a significant decision you made in your personal life: for example, choosing a holiday, applying for a job or selecting some items to buy for your home.

- Did you research your purchase before making it, asking family, friends, associates or checking reviews?

- Why do you need the item? Do you need it now? What is the risk involved? Will your purchase meet your needs?

- Do you have the required documents, licences or means to purchase it?

- Are there any alternatives?

- Reflect on your decision; was it the right one?

Congratulations, you have applied a decision-making process to a common scenario. Add proportionality and necessity (Chapter 7) to the calculations and you are prepared to use the NDM in policing situations.

The importance of investigative decision making is illustrated by Irving and Dunninghan (1993), who found that the most common factor in the failure of investigations is 'flawed decision making'. Investigations and decision making require accountability, initially through the justice system and more widely where professionalism may be questioned. Investigators will be called upon to rationalise, justify and prove objectivity in their decision making. Adherence to the recommended model will ensure officers are supported, in the event that their decisions are questioned or where subsequent discoveries would have altered the decision if the situation had been known at the time. Investigative decisions tend to be acute when made in dynamic situations, as represented by golden hour principles, or considered where time is available to consider all influences and ramifications. The NDM is equally applicable to both situations.

Decisions can be based on the interpretation of material. The material must be evaluated regarding its usefulness or otherwise, which is examined next.

POLICING SPOTLIGHT

Areas popular with tourists attract criminals, who target people on holiday. Cars contain more property than usual with occupants relaxed in their holiday mode. This led to a steep rise in thefts from cars in a national park area during the 1980s. Intensive enquiries were based around observations and checks of suspicious people and vehicles. These were largely ineffective for many weeks until a successful vehicle check led to the two offenders being arrested. It transpired that the two elderly disabled offenders had been sighted many times but were discounted from the enquiry because of their appearance by a series of officers. This provides an example of satisficing: subjective hypothesis and bias in decision making. As a detective you should embrace the phrase that things are not always what they seem!

EVALUATION

Evaluation features in both the stages of an investigation and the investigative mindset, as detailed in Chapter 2. Determining the value of the material you have collected is important for the direction of your investigation and decision making. In your experience of decision making, you will have used and discarded information to inform your choices.

In order to employ this technique in an investigative context, you should take a critical, questioning approach, as emphasised in the ABC model (Core Investigative Doctrine: ACPO, 2012a).

- **A**ssume nothing

- **B**elieve nothing

- **C**hallenge everything

The information you are relying on must be truthful and accurate. You should start with the provenance of the information, to borrow from the intelligence world. Is the source of the information reliable, unreliable or unknown? How did the source know the information? (This is equally applicable to digital sources.) Can you corroborate the material through other sources?

HYPOTHESES AND INFERENCES

Examining clues allows you to draw inferences about the actions and actors associated with the criminal event you are investigating. An inference represents a conclusion based on evidence; for example, you discover a knife with bloodstains during a search following a stabbing – an inference would be that this was the weapon used. You will then create lines of enquiry to confirm the inference and gain evidence to prove it. Innes (2007) proposes that investigation is a constructive process concerned with reducing uncertainty. These uncertainties thrive where gaps exist. This is where employing a hypothesis will aid your investigation. A hypothesis is a possible answer to a question, not a guess. It is based on objective, rational logic representing the most likely answer to incomplete explanations uncovered in your investigation. In science you would test a hypothesis by experimentation; in a criminal investigation you investigate it. Not all investigations require a hypothesis; if you can factually explain the situation, a hypothesis would be irrational. An open-minded approach in accordance with the investigative mindset is recommended throughout investigations. Information may indicate a suspect at an early stage, but where this does not occur, a well-developed hypothesis is recommended. A hypothesis is a suggested explanation for a group of facts. Your analysis will be influenced by experience and tacit knowledge; however, you should take care that bias (as introduced in Chapter 2) does not affect your independent approach to hypothesis creation, which must be objective in nature. The hypothesis is dependent on your analysis and understanding of all available information; the suggested explanation will lead to further lines of enquiry to support or weaken your theory. The 5WH approach (see Table 3.1) recommended by Stelfox (2012) is helpful in recognising what is known and what knowledge gaps exist. You should ask yourself the following questions.

- Do you know exactly what happened; if not, where will you seek the missing information?

- When did this happen? Many offences are classified as occurring between two times, which can be lengthy. What can you do to make this more precise?

- Where did it happen? This may be along a route or between a number of locations.

- Who is the victim, witnesses and suspects? How can you identify them?

- Why did the event occur? What can your enquiries bring to the scenario to explain what happened?

Further lines of enquiry will be required to challenge your hypothesis. Additional information coupled with your application of reasoning will support or negate your suggestions.

Table 3.1 5WH approach

	What do you know?	What do you not know?
What?		
When?		
Where?		
Who?		
Why?		
How?		

You will start to identify consistencies and contradictions; this is a natural part of the investigative process which will identify new lines of enquiry. If you do not feel equipped to analyse the information, consider engaging with others as discussed in Chapter 6. A hypothesis should be accompanied by an investigative plan with objectives designed to achieve your aim of confirming the hypothesis or providing an alternative. The following section aims to make sense of reasoning. A final thought before moving on: do not over-complicate your hypothesis development; when in doubt, keep it simple.

REASONING

An open-minded methodical approach to reasoning and analysis maximises your investigative prowess. Logical thinking allows you to construct a picture from fragments of information. Bryant (2009) argues that reasoning skills are the key to intelligence analysis. Reasoning can be sub-divided into two types: inductive and deductive. This is worthy of some explanation. The fictional detective Sherlock Holmes famously 'deduces' explanations from his observations. DiYanni (2016) explains that Holmes actually follows a hybrid inductive–deductive pathway, drawing inferences from observations combined with logical reasoning. Holmes discards material he believes irrelevant to achieve his hypothesis in an inductive manner; he then applies deductive reasoning to the situation. Figure 3.3 shows the differences between the two approaches.

SPECIFIC ↓ GENERAL	**INDUCTIVE**	**DEDUCTIVE**	GENERAL ↓ SPECIFIC
	Observations	Hypothesis	
	Inferences	Inference	
	Hypothesis	Confirmation	

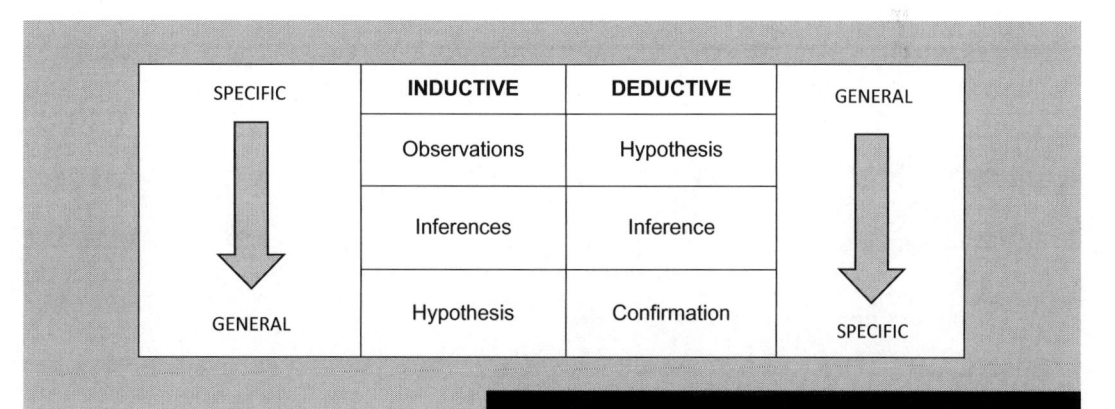

Figure 3.3 Inductive versus deductive reasoning

Having concentrated on analysing and evaluating your material, it is time to move to strategies. Investigative strategies allow you to consider variables and influences in a longer-term approach that is rarely available in the early dynamic stages of your enquiries. Some commonly employed investigative strategies will now be explored.

HOUSE-TO-HOUSE STRATEGIES

House-to-house (H2H) enquiries are an efficient way of achieving an array of objectives. The early stages of any investigation often result in 'fast-track' H2H. Fast-track enquiries will not be as focused as later similar actions; however, there is no reason for speed to equal a lack of professionalism.

The Association of Chief Police Officers (2006a) suggest three objectives for H2H enquiry:

- identifying suspects;

- identifying witnesses;

- gathering information and intelligence.

The opportunity to offer personal and community reassurance can also be added to this list.

Prior to conducting any H2H enquiries, the parameters of the enquiry should be established. The mnemonic LEASH is a useful reminder for setting fast-track parameters.

- **L**ain in wait.

- **E**gress routes.

- **A**ccess routes.

- **S**ight.

- **H**earing.

Could the occupants assist with information gleaned from their proximity to the crime scene or event?

As with all aspects of an investigation, an intelligence-led approach is recommended. When designing an H2H strategy it is beneficial to consider local and community intelligence and awareness of local issues. You should also consider that householders will view the enquiring investigators as representative of law enforcement and may use the contact as an opportunity to raise unconnected matters; therefore, a strategic response should be part of the H2H design. Known offenders living in the area and the linguistic or cultural needs of a community are all helpful to the enquiry.

A structured approach is suggested, and asking the right questions is an important facet of the enquiry. It would be preferable for all householders to be asked the same questions rather than adopting an ad-hoc approach dependent on the individual investigator. The same approach should be taken to information of reassurance provided, as the householders will undoubtedly speak to each other and possibly to the press. If mixed messages are provided this will reflect on the professionalism of your investigation.

The design of wider H2H enquiries may benefit from reference to the mnemonic LEAVERS.

- **L**ast seen

- **E**ncounter site

- **A**ttack site

- **V**ictim frequented locations

- **E**vidence and dump sites

- **R**outes to and/or from

- **S**ites and proximities of witnesses

As mentioned earlier, H2H represents an opportunity to engage with communities, and the prospect of gaining information based on the ABC principle outlined in Chapter 2 should not be missed. The H2H investigators should consider compiling the following information during their H2H actions:

- description of interviewee;

- vehicles;

- movements;

- verification/corroboration of information;

- clothing;

- knowledge of victim/scene;

- any other information including the enquiring investigators' thoughts and opinions.

The views and opinions of all members of an investigative team should be gathered. A trait of effective investigators is the encouragement they provide to others to share their thoughts and findings.

The H2H enquiry should not be seen as a 'tick-box' element of the investigation; the information obtained will be of most benefit when assimilated and combined with all other sources to provide the fullest picture possible. Your strategy should also include a plan for revisiting addresses should no response be received. You should decide if you only need to speak to a representative from the address or all occupants, and then build your strategy around the identified aims. The following critical thinking activity shows what a member of the public experiences when enquiries are not well constructed.

CRITICAL THINKING ACTIVITY 3.1

LEVEL 4

I (Iain Stainton) have recently experienced house-to-house enquiries from the public's point of view. Together with my neighbours I was visited by an officer who informed us 'something serious had happened in the area the previous evening', asking if we had seen anything. When asked what the incident was, they replied that it was confidential, and they were not at liberty to explain. Neither my neighbours nor I had any knowledge of an incident and were unable to add anything. The visits from the police led to a general feeling of unease in the neighbourhood, generating local gossip but no useful information.

Compare what you have read of house-to-house enquiries with this real-life example. Do you feel this was a proficient way to conduct such enquiries? How would you approach the same situation?

MEDIA STRATEGIES

Reading any newspaper or engaging with news media, either local or national, reveals the amount of crime featuring in the news. The 24-hour news and social media environment which currently predominates society requires an updated approach of the traditional investigative management of media strategies, which tended to concentrate on serious and high-profile investigations. The increase in citizen journalism, as members of the public create material through social media, requires an understanding of media influence throughout policing.

The Leveson enquiry (2012) recognised some police–press relationships, finding that some dealings were inappropriate. This led to a culture of accountability in police–media contacts.

The public represent one of the most fruitful sources of information to the investigator, as illustrated by the *Crimewatch* (1984–2016) television series. The media are a vital source in ensuring the widest possible coverage for appeals and information directed to the public. Marsh and Melville (2014) advise that the police must be prepared for the amount of information media appeals can generate, as shown in point 4 of the decision-making section of this chapter.

The College of Policing's Authorised Professional Practice on media relations (2021a) makes the point that a successful working relationship between the police and media is an important element of investigations, and the enhanced communications this relationship provides helps to solve crime and reassure communities. Media strategies will help you to:

- identify offenders;
- locate suspects;
- identify victims;
- trace and locate witnesses;
- provide reassurance.

The instant nature of social media necessitates a fast-track response that traditional press conferences did not require. Photo and video coverage, commentary and opinion all have the potential to contaminate investigative material; for example, are witnesses conveying their memories or repeating what they have accessed? Identifying parties to a crime in this manner has a number of negative ramifications, including alerting offenders to their identification, corrupting identifications or, in the worst-case scenario, encouraging vigilante activity. You should take steps to counter this type of information by providing general information such as a general location, the nature of the incident, any warnings you think are pertinent and reassurance that the matter is receiving attention. The majority of police forces maintain their own social media accounts, which can be used to counter public coverage over which you have little control.

Longer-term media strategies will see you addressing the following areas.

- Privacy: Seek the consent of victims before publicising their details. Arrested persons should not be named unless a legitimate reason for doing so exists; where such a reason is identified, refer to senior officers for guidance before naming people.

- Where a suspect has been identified and is not traced, give consideration to publicising this to assist in locating them. Take care not to breach PACE Code D guidelines, which may undermine identifications.

- Witness appeals: These should be coordinated to maximise effect. Locations, times and basic details of the event will support focused appeals.

- Reassurance should be given where appropriate to avoid inducing fears or panics. Include preventative suggestions, ensuring your reassurance is credible. Avoid stressing how rare an event is if there have been a series of similar incidents in the location. Credibility is easily lost.

Contacts between investigators and the media should be recorded in your notes, and the College of Policing stress that the police code of ethics should be considered alongside your media strategy (College of Policing, 2021a). You should take care in your own use of social media, for example avoiding commenting on crime matters, as a number of officers have fallen foul of this in discipline matters in the recent past. It is important to remember that the media is a valuable resource, not an opponent. As with any multi-agency response, you must understand and re-enforce your preferred terms of engagement at the outset. A well-designed media strategy represents the best-possible chance to obtain public coverage of your appeal or message.

CRITICAL THINKING ACTIVITY 3.2

LEVEL 6

Choose a selection of news sources, newspapers, online sources or television news reports, ideally representing a variety of types of coverage. What proportion is devoted to crime?

Select a specific event which is reported across news sources. How do the various sources report the same news? Evaluate any variance you have discovered and then summarise why this occurs.

TIE STRATEGIES

The abbreviation TIE is effectively an instruction directing investigators to trace, interview and eliminate individuals or groups of people featuring in an investigation.

As your investigation progresses, you will identify groups to enquire into further: this may be to identify suspects or witnesses. TIE (Trace, Interview, Eliminate, or sometimes Trace, Implicate, Evaluate) strategies were introduced following the Yorkshire Ripper enquiry in 1985 (see Chapter 9). These strategies represent an objective way of concentrating on eliminating group members who are not implicated, allowing you to focus on those who are, with the ultimate aim of identifying suspects or witnesses.

One way of viewing this is that the investigator starts with a group of people, which they must prune until they are left with a perpetrator. Wright et al (2015) explain that alongside suspect strategies, TIE actions tend to be the most significant, intrusive and consuming in terms of time and resources within an enquiry. This confirms the importance of understanding this investigative technique.

The Core Investigative Doctrine (ACPO, 2012a) explains that a TIE category is a group of people sharing a common characteristic, which is likely to include the offender or witness. The common characteristic will depend on the circumstances. TIE categories are typically but not exhaustively based upon:

- those with access to the scene at the time of the offence;

- those living within or associated with a certain geographic area;

- those associated with the victim;

- those with previous convictions of similarity;

- those with physical characteristics similar to the offender;

- those with access to certain types of vehicle.

The TIE category then requires populating. Once the criteria have been decided, people fitting the criteria must be identified to facilitate the enquiry.

For example, imagine an assault takes place in a public house, and in the first instance investigators would like to speak to all who were present to gain information and identify offenders. How would you identify who had been in the pub? You might look at the following sources:

- records kept;

- CCTV;

- databases;

- appeals.

These are all worthy options. 'Snowballing' gathers material and focuses the criteria as the investigation progresses. For example, you trace and speak to a witness, who refers to other people who were present, who in turn refer to others thus increasing the number of people who may have information in the same way a snowball gets bigger collecting more snow as it rolls

The victim of the assault describes a male; can you eliminate any females in the premises at the time? Bear in mind you are eliminating people as offenders, not witnesses. The male was wearing a red football shirt. Does this give you further options in focusing the group? Following this technique may produce more manageable enquiries.

As an investigation progresses offender characteristics may become more apparent, for example:

- sex;

- age;

- physical characteristics;

- fingerprints;

- forensic characteristics such as DNA, footprints, fibres;

- vehicle ownership/access;

- clothing.

Any of these can influence the forming of a TIE category. Context is also important: for example, ownership of a red shirt is less indicative of a specific individual than DNA.

Wright et al (2015) recommend a format for use in TIE enquiries, and suggest that the enquiring investigator should consider the following criteria.

- Why is the individual a TIE?

- What are their antecedents (convictions, intelligence)?

- What are their movements during relevant times?

- What is their association with the victim?

- What is their alibi?

- What was their behavioural pattern prior to the event?

- Are there forensics?

- Are there inconsistencies?

- Did the person have the motive to commit the offence?

- Did the person have the opportunity to commit the offence?

- Did the person have the means to commit the offence?

- What is the investigator's opinion?

The Byford report (1981), which features in the following policing spotlight and Chapter 9, highlighted a number of missed opportunities to identify a suspect in TIE-style enquiries.

POLICING SPOTLIGHT

Between 1975 and 1980, 13 women were murdered in northern England. The investigation, known as the 'Yorkshire Ripper' enquiry, led to the conviction of Peter Sutcliffe. The sheer size of the investigation was breathtaking. Part of the investigation, such as identifying the recipients of bank notes, brought 8000 people into a TIE line of enquiry. 53,000 vehicle owners needed to be traced and interviewed. At the time of Sutcliffe's arrest, 36,000 documents were awaiting processing in the incident room (which had to be moved as the weight of documents was weakening the floors of the original police station). The Byford report into the investigation (explored in Chapter 9) was critical of a variety of elements, including the manner in which investigators moved from one line of enquiry to another without concluding the original. The most infamous of these was the concentration on letters and recordings purporting to be from the offender, which transpired to be hoaxes. Byford led to the creation of Major Incident Room Standardised Administration Procedures (MIRSAP) and the Home Office Large Major Enquiry System (HOLMES), which support major enquiries to this day. When using TIE strategies, ensure you complete the enquiry before disregarding it. If it merited a line of enquiry in the first place, then that line needs to be followed to a conclusion.

Eliminating people from an enquiry is as important as implicating them. Suspect identification is an objective process and it must follow that elimination criteria should also be objective. An acceptable form of elimination from the enquiry is of equal importance to your initial construction of the criteria. The *Murder Investigation Manual* (ACPO, 2006b) suggests the following series of elimination criteria which investigators can choose from when creating TIE strategies.

- **Forensic elimination:** If forensic comparison material is available, forensic comparison may be considered. Powers to obtain forensic samples from members of the public must be considered in this area.

- **Description:** Where a description is available from earlier enquiries, parameters could be set from analysis of the description. As with all material the credibility of the description must be considered.

- **Alibi:** Provision of an account for salient points is an inherent part of a TIE strategy. It is likely that any alibi would be investigated to confirm them or otherwise. This leads to sub-divisions for acceptable alibis. These are provided by independent witnesses (confirmed by passive data generators), associates, relatives, spouse or partner. These criteria should be confirmed in advance rather than an ad-hoc response to developing events in a strategic manner.

- **Not eliminated:** A strategy must consider all eventualities, in this case including a person not being eliminated from the enquiry. This does not necessarily lead to a person being declared a suspect but will likely require further investigations as the situation will probably transcend the circumstances leading to their inclusion as a TIE.

SUSPECTS

Identifying a suspect or suspects is a significant stage of the investigation, as outlined in Chapter 2. The impact of categorising a person as a 'suspect' and the legislative ramifications this brings are substantial. Even when following legal guidelines, misjudging arrest reactions can have significant ramifications, such as jeopardising the credibility of investigations. This was illustrated by the case *Sir Cliff Richard v The BBC & The Chief Constable of South Yorkshire Police* [2018] EWHC 1837, which saw damages awarded when media coverage of an arrest exceeded the balance between privacy and public interest.

Identifying suspects is reliant on a wealth of investigative techniques, victim and witnesses accounts, forensic support, intelligence surveillance and TIE.

It is possible that an arrest may arise from a dynamic situation, allowing little time for planning. This is where an overall professional knowledge base and understanding of discretionary powers will benefit the investigator.

The decision to designate a suspect effectively creates a risk assessment situation. You should always ask yourself if an arrest is necessary, and if you decide it is, powers of arrest cater for taking individuals into custody. You must decide the appropriate time and strategy. If it is felt that investigations should continue to gather material, ask yourself if it is appropriate or indeed safe to leave an identified suspect in the community. Will they interfere with evidence/witnesses, flee or commit further offences? Risk, resources and logistics should all also be considered. The legality of arrest is addressed in section 24 of PACE, with necessity criteria introduced by section 110 of the Serious Organised Crime and Police Act 2005.

A suspect can be held in custody for 24 hours, and to hold a person longer than this requires authority from a senior officer (maximum 12 hours) and subsequently by a magistrate up to a maximum of 96 hours without a person being charged. You can plan for the likely eventualities of custody time limits in your suspect strategy.

A person in custody will be given an opportunity to comment on the allegations in the form of an interview. Interview strategies (see Chapter 5) will be created to inform the interview process, including analysis of what material will be introduced in the interview, and at what point it is vital.

It is important to realise that, following an arrest, time in custody is limited and this should inform any arrest strategy. Other considerations should include the following questions.

- What offence do you propose they are arrested for?

- What time and venue is best for the arrest?

- How will the arrest be conducted?

- Have you considered searches?

- Which facility will they be taken to?

- If there are multiple suspects, will you use the same custody suite for all?

- Do you require forensic samples from the detained person?

- Do you have legal powers to obtain samples?

- What are the likely effects of the arrest on the victim, witnesses, community and the detained person's family?

- Do you envisage media attention?

- Do you have the resources to action quick time enquiries which may arise?

Where you identify one of the above or other concerns, you must devise a plan for dealing with it.

At this stage, it is important to review your investigation to date to identify any lines of enquiry remaining open. Do you feel you have sufficient material to justify your proposed actions? An arrest is a significant stage but does not represent the end of an investigation. This may be the first time to gain a suspect's account or conduct searches. You may have to review any findings so far, and new lines of enquiry are likely to occur as a result. As with every part of an investigation, the suspect strategy should merge with all other elements to create one single entity.

Advice on the following additional strategies can be found by referring to the appropriate chapter.

- Witness and victims – Chapter 4.

- Interviewing – Chapter 5.

- Passive data generators – Chapter 6.

- Covert activities – Chapter 7.

- Community – Chapter 8.

- Disclosure – Chapter 9.

SUMMARY OF KEY CONCEPTS

This chapter builds on the investigative foundations of Chapter 2. The content equips you to:

- demonstrate your understanding of decision making through your practice;

- use TIE strategies;

- evaluate investigative material;

- produce investigative strategies.

CHECK YOUR KNOWLEDGE

1. Explain how you would use 'snowballing' when constructing TIE categories.

2. You are investigating a theft of a games console where a suspect has been identified. You arrested them and searched premises with no trace of the stolen property. The suspect makes no comment in the interview. What possible hypothesis can you draw from this situation?

3. An assault has taken place at the centre of your town's night-time economy area. How will material attrition impact on your information gathering?

4. Evaluate the strengths and weaknesses of the TIE elimination criteria.

Sample answers to these questions are provided at the end of the book.

FURTHER READING

Rogers, C (2011) *Police Work: Principles and Practice*. Abingdon: Routledge.
This practitioner's view of policing links community, investigation and intelligence elements, explaining how one complements the other.

Wright, M, Cook, T, Pinder, D, Gregory, A and Shaw, G (2015) T.I.E. Practice, Terminology, Tactics and Training. *The Journal of Homicide and Major Incident Investigation*, 10(2).
This article explores TIE strategies at a thought-provoking level.

CHAPTER 4
WITNESS AND VICTIM MANAGEMENT

LEARNING OBJECTIVES

AFTER READING THIS CHAPTER YOU WILL BE ABLE TO:

- understand how the investigation approach works in relation to witnesses using case examples;

- understand how vulnerable or intimidated witnesses may be categorised by investigators;

- understand the law and some case studies around vulnerable or intimidated witnesses;

- recall the rights of victims under the Victim Code.

INTRODUCTION

This chapter examines and considers approaches to witnesses in the criminal justice system, with a focus on the investigative work undertaken during criminal investigations. Understanding the laws, policies and processes around witnesses will aid investigators by increasing the likelihood that the investigation will be fair in relation to witnesses, but also that reasonable lines of enquiry from witness evidence will be progressed and the witnesses' evidence will be admissible in later criminal proceedings.

WITNESSES: UNDERSTANDING THE INITIAL INVESTIGATION APPROACH

The central principle within many adversarial justice systems is that of orality, where a witness gives an oral account of the events they have witnessed. Witnesses in criminal trials, as both victims and non-victims, are relied upon to provide evidence (Cook and Tattersall, 2010). It is usual for the witness to first relay their account to the police, and for it to be noted down, in a first account or a written witness statement (Criminal Justice Act 1967, s 9; Magistrates Court Act 1980, ss 5A (3) (a) and 5B; Criminal Procedure Rules 2005, Rule 27.1). Witnesses observe many areas of both private and public spaces and at every stage in criminal proceedings all persons are (whatever their age) competent to give evidence (Youth Justice and Criminal Evidence Act 1999, s 53). A witness, by simple explanation, is someone who sees something happen and can describe it themselves.

In private spaces, investigators might find that witnesses, for example of domestic abuse or child abuse, are often far fewer in number than those in public spaces. In public spaces, witnesses may be more abundant, so investigators may find themselves receiving many accounts and reviewing those which are relevant to the case being investigated or require the investigator to undertake further reasonable lines of enquiry. In either scenario, the investigator must be diligent to avoid witness evidence being missed or being recorded poorly, resulting in key details about the case potentially being lost. The policing spotlight example on page 67 concerning the John Jones case will give some context to this. Speaking with witnesses during the early stages of an investigation may yield a large amount of detail about the immediate events the witness has seen; however, there are some important considerations to be made about both the timing of the gathering of this evidence and the way the evidence is obtained. In early investigation phases, or when trying to determine what a number of witnesses have seen, the accounts obtained by investigators are 'initial accounts' and usually these accounts are vital to understand some of the first comments and observations made by witnesses (College of Policing, 2021b). These first accounts may also be important evidence, or the only evidence available, in cases where a witness's evidence is introduced later as hearsay evidence (a form of evidence admissible under certain conditions; see the Criminal Justice Act 2003 on statutory gateways). The first accounts may be further explored during later, and perhaps in more detailed and formal, stages of an investigation.

Some basic principles concerning first accounts are as follows.

1. Build rapport with witnesses early and avoid determining the value of a witness's evidence without first considering what evidence they have to offer. This rapport may lead to the witness having more confidence to report important or sensitive information.

2. Separate witnesses physically to avoid contaminating one witness's evidence with another. This is really important as sometimes a witness's evidence could become contaminated simply because they become confused between what they have seen and what others have seen.

3. Obtain first accounts even when a witness appears intoxicated; this account may be impacted by the further consumption of alcohol or sleep. A first account can be revisited, but a failure to take a first account may result in no account being available at all.

4. Allow for some uncertainty, and only use open questioning approaches with the witness leading their own account and recall, prompted by limited questions. First accounts are often obtained following traumatic events, and sometimes distressed witnesses can be confused, so allow for some uncertainty but ensure an account is recorded.

5. Clarify sources of information to the witness, or other witnesses who may have witnessed the same event. In any case, ensure that the witness's details are correctly obtained. Without clarity over who the witness has seen and how the witness has seen the events, this may lead to confusion about the evidence the witness might give.

6. Record any demeanour, reluctance or physical communication needs alongside any self-stated vulnerabilities the witnesses may provide. This information is vital for future evidence gathering and deciding how to approach witnesses in the future.

7. The initial recall and account should be completed within 24 hours of an incident and under these conditions; the beneficial impact of early recall on long-term memory endures for at least one month.

(Chevroulet et al, 2021; College of Policing, 2020b)

You will not be able to understand some of the basics around obtaining first accounts from witnesses. However, what is vitally important is that witnesses' first accounts are accurate and allow the witness a chance to express what they have seen in the best way possible. An example of research around autistic witnesses describes how some accounts may at first appear scrambled and illogical; however, the investigator needs to work with this to ensure accurate details are recalled.

EVIDENCE-BASED POLICING

Autistic people may provide information which may appear disorganised or that the witness is jumping between topics and the narrative is scrambled. A study of 33 autistic and 30 typically developing participants were interviewed about their memory for two videos depicting criminal events (Maras et al, 2020). Clip segments of one video were 'scrambled', disrupting the event's narrative structure; the other video was watched intact. Both autistic and non-autistic witnesses recalled fewer details with less accuracy from the scrambled video, and a witness-aimed first account structure revealed a more accurate recall. In a witness-aimed first account structure, the interviewer accepts that the account might not follow an expected sequence and a group of topics or individual topics might need to be revisited. However, unlike usual free recalls of an event, some topics are simply labelled for the person to see; therefore, this allows them to come back to this area. This study also found that removing the narrative structure of an event had a profound effect on recall. Using and sharing your note taking with a witness may help them to sequence, recall and be more accurate about the account they are providing.

Now consider the following policing spotlight feature, which outlines an assault. Within this example you should consider your approach to the witness, named John, and consider what you now know about first accounts.

After reading this section, you should have a good understanding of first accounts and initial investigation concerning witnesses. Some key takeaways are as follows.

1. Always consider a first account during the initial stages of an investigation.

2. Take steps to determine the vulnerability of any witness.

3. Don't rely on the type of crime to determine the response: judge each witness and the circumstances on their merits.

4. Communicate clearly any vulnerability identified and first account obtained to any further investigation team.

POLICING SPOTLIGHT

THE CASE OF JOHN JONES

Now that you have begun to think about witnesses in the criminal justice system, you should be able to understand how an investigator might respond to an incident where witnesses are present. Read the following witness case example – John Jones:

> *John was making his way home on the bus; it was early in the evening and there was still fairly good visibility. After disembarking from the bus, he saw two people having an argument before one punched the other in the face, causing him to fall to the floor. John made his way over, but before getting there two police officers arrived. John provided his name to the officers and indicated that he had witnessed the punch.*

Think now about this case, and how the investigation might be undertaken and where an investigator might begin. Some of the initial considerations from the John Jones case might be the following.

1. John is a witness to the assault. You may need to obtain a first account from him and record this so that he is able to review and sign it. Some police forces also have specialist booklets for first accounts and others may use a digital device. However the witness's account and details are recorded, they must be saved in a durable format so they can be revisited at a later date.

2. John may be asked if he can provide a first account of what he has seen, and you should use the principles set out by the College of Policing.

3. The officers will need John's contact details if they are to recontact him. Remember that witness contact details are personal information and may not be revealed to anyone without proper regard to the rules around disclosure in criminal cases. It is also important that these details are shared with anyone who might further investigate the case on your behalf or supervise the case.

4. If John's bus has external CCTV then this may show the assault. Gathering evidence like CCTV and accounts from other witnesses is important. This evidence could support John's account in the future, and this is part of the investigator's requirement to follow reasonable lines of enquiry in the case.

In this case, the arrival of the police was fairly quick, and from this John was able to speak with the officers at the scene. However, if John had made his way home then the investigators may have needed to issue a 'press release' about the incident to prompt any witnesses to call them. The investigators may also hand this case over to other investigation teams and so it's important that references about the case are included, like an incident or enquiry reference.

> John informs the officers that he is on his way home from college, which he attends for help with his reading and writing. John is unable to read the first account the investigator has obtained and asks for it to be read aloud to him. John says that sometimes he struggles with words and the time so wasn't sure that the incident lasted for 15 minutes.

The information provided by John is the first indication that he is likely to need support if he is to be called to support the case in the future. If there was a failure to record information about John's vulnerabilities then this may lead to his evidence being obtained incorrectly or without consideration of the support needed for John.

CRITICAL THINKING ACTIVITY 4.1

LEVEL 4

Review the John Jones case above and identify answers to the following questions.

1. Why should John's vulnerabilities be documented alongside his account?

2. How could John's initial account be used later in the case?

3. What enquiry could be undertaken to help generate other witnesses in John's case?

4. What rights does John have in respect of being a witness?

Sample answers to these questions are provided at the end of the book.

A CASE STUDY: R VERSUS IQBAL

Now that you have been able to understand John's case, and some of the initial actions you might consider for his case, you should read the following case of *R v Iqbal*. In this example you will see one of the consequences of failing to recognise the support needed for some witnesses.

During an investigation concerning the circumstances of an assault, the investigators obtained a statement from the victim, who was returning from a course at a local college. The victim had been assaulted by two men, one of whom was in possession of a knuckle duster. The assault caused the victim to become unconscious for a period of time. The police obtained a number of statements from the victim. The men suspected of the assault were charged. The trial was later halted after it became obvious that the victim could not understand certain questions; a report later highlighted that the victim had significant impairment of social functioning, intelligence and communication, appearing more competent in language and communication skills than he actually was. The victim did not necessarily show or indicate any lack of understanding, nor was he asked about this during any taking of accounts from him. That left people to overestimate the victim's understanding and ability to process all parts of a series of questions accurately. Although the victim had a good understanding of everyday spoken language, understanding of complex and embedded questions was inconsistent. Furthermore, the victim did not spontaneously describe being incapable of understanding, willing instead to be seen as capable and not to draw attention to the difficulties experienced. The victim in this case should have been provided with special measures to assist him and his needs should have been recognised by the investigator from the outset of the case.

SPECIAL MEASURES

The term 'special measures' refers to measures used to provide a witness with assistance in court. However, the determination that special measures might be required must begin at the very start of the investigation. The Youth Justice and Criminal Evidence Act 1999 (YJCEA) was designed, in part, to assist the witness in the task of giving evidence to the courts, placing between witnesses and the court a support mechanism to alleviate fear and enable some witnesses with psychological vulnerabilities, or those victim to sexual crimes and other serious offences, measures such as screens and video-recorded evidence (Hoyle and Zedner, 2007; Cook and Tattersall, 2010; Durston, 2011). It did not remove orally testified evidence but did change the way in which it is delivered to the court, and therefore changed the approach which needs to be taken within the investigation and by the investigation team. This may include recording a witness's evidence on video.

> ## REFLECTIVE PRACTICE 4.1
> ### LEVEL 4
>
> Consider again the John Jones case study on page 67. Do you think John may need to be considered for special measures?

The Youth Justice and Criminal Evidence Act 1999 was largely enacted on evidence from the Pigot Report (1989) and the Youth Justice and Criminal Evidence Act 1999 (Baber, 1999). The enacted measures under the YJCEA are:

- screening from the defendant (section 23);

- evidence by live link (section 24);

- evidence given in private (section 25);

- removal of wigs and gowns (section 26);

- video-recorded evidence in chief (section 27);

- video-recorded cross-examination or re-examination (section 28);

- examination of witness through an intermediary (section 29);

- aids to communication (section 30).

It was reported in the 1999 House of Commons Green Paper (Baber, 1999) that the implementation of special measures was at odds with the principle of orality (Roberts and Zuckerman, 2010). A Home Office working group intended the outcome of the 1999 act to be to deal with vulnerable and intimidated witnesses, specifically redressing the balance between protecting the principles of a fair trial and ensuring that witnesses, particularly those in sexual cases, were not unduly disadvantaged (Baber, 1999). Police training will often cover the YJCEA as a subject within their focus on achieving best evidence (ABE). The term ABE is also often used to describe a series of actions taken to assist victims and witnesses to give their best-possible evidence; it was first described by the Home Office and used as language for guidance around victims and witnesses (Home Office, 2000; Macpherson, 2001). The term ABE should not simply be used to describe a video-recorded interview, as this is only one of a possible number of options for witnesses. The term video-recorded evidence (VRE) may be used to describe where a video recording of a witnesses account has been obtained.

WHY ARE SPECIAL MEASURES IMPORTANT?

The YJCEA enables witnesses to give evidence which may otherwise not be entered into the Criminal Court, either because the witness is too afraid or because they are unable to offer evidence without an intermediary or aids to communication (Macpherson, 2001). Through the YJCEA, special measures are offered to witnesses on an individual basis and can be granted through an application to the court during a criminal trial (Durston, 2011; Ewin, 2016). There are three main issues, which are:

1. the identification process for vulnerable and intimidated witnesses within the investigation phase, with some opportunities being missed to identify witnesses who need support (Ellison, 1999; Burton et al, 2006; Charles, 2012);

2. communication channels between the investigator and the courts, which sometimes results in some measures being lost or abandoned and special measures being unsuccessful (Burton et al, 2006; Criminal Justice Joint Inspectorate, 2009);

3. evidence-gathering opportunities to support witnesses who may need assistance from an intermediary, or having their evidence obtained by way of video-recorded interview, are missed in some investigations (Denyer, 2011; MoJ, 2011; O'Mahony et al, 2011; Charles, 2012; Doak and McGourlay, 2012).

Investigators also need to decide between the two main gateways within the YJCEA for witnesses, and courts will then approve measures based on the assessment provided from the investigation. The two gateways are as follows.

- **Section 16.** Witnesses eligible for assistance on grounds of age or incapacity. This is often referred to as being for vulnerable witnesses. This section covers witnesses who are under 18, or suffer from a mental, intelligence or social impairment, or physical disability. This section also covers persons with a mental disorder in accordance with the Mental Health Act 1983.

- **Section 17.** Witnesses eligible for assistance on grounds of fear or distress about testifying. This is often referred to as being for intimidated witnesses. This section covers witnesses who may be intimidated by the accused due to their behaviour or are a victim of a sexual or modern slavery offence. This gateway is wider than section 16, and potentially is open to more witnesses, providing the investigator assesses the needs of the witness appropriately.

This chapter will now explore the case of *R v PR* [2010] in a case study. This case is important because it emphasises the need to consider carefully which gateway under the YJCEA is important. In the *R v PR* case, the witness was believed to require special measures under section 17 of the act; however, vital information was missing from the assessment of the witness, who required measures under section 16 of the YJCEA.

CASE STUDY: R VERSUS PR

In *R v PR* [2010] EWCA Crim 2741, it was recorded that the victim of historic familial rape was permitted special measures under the gateway of fear and distress of testifying (YJCEA 1999, s 17). The section 17 gateway allows witnesses to receive special measures on the grounds of their social, cultural and ethnic origin; domestic and employment circumstances; religious beliefs; political opinions; or behaviour towards the witness by the accused, their family or associates; or that they are the complainant in a 'sexual' case (Doak and McGourlay, 2012). Arguably, the section 17 gateway is less well used by investigators and the courts, and largely this falls down to identification of witnesses who are eligible for special measures (Roberts and Zuckerman, 2010). In *R v PR*, it was not identified that the victim-witness also had a learning disability, resulting in an inability to comprehend complex questions, highlighting a misidentification between so-called intimidated witnesses (YJCEA 1999, s 17) and vulnerable witnesses (YJCEA 1999, s 16).

CRITICAL THINKING ACTIVITY 4.2

LEVEL 4

Having read the above section, you should now be able to describe the difference between section 16 and section 17 of the YJCEA. Try and answer these questions in reference to the previous case study.

1. What is the appropriate gateway for the witness?

2. Have the views of the witness been considered?

3. What are the measures available to assist witnesses?

INTERMEDIARIES AND SPECIAL MEASURES

One of the areas which has a significant impact for vulnerable and intimidated witnesses is section 29 of the YJCEA, where an intermediary can be present to assist a witness or the defendant in giving evidence, or in understanding the proceedings (O'Mahony et al, 2011). Intermediaries are agents of the court and their role is independent of either counsel: they are present to service the communication needs of whoever needs their support. Despite their importance, there is an underestimation of the prevalence of communication problems among vulnerable and intimidated witnesses. In conjunction, an overestimation of competence is also observed, characterised by assumptions that advocates, and in some cases investigators, know best, and it has been found that they use ill-informed toolkits as an assessment frameworks, and do not consider intermediaries for defendants (Plotnikoff and Woolfson, 2007; O'Mahony, 2013; Henderson, 2015; Ewin, 2016; O'Mahony et al, 2016). Under the YJCEA, a judge may grant special measures to assist with communication difficulties in respect of vulnerable defendants (*R v Camberwell Green Youth Court* [2005] UKHL 4; European Court of Human Rights (ECtHR) in *SC v UK* [2004] ECHR 263, [2005] FCR 347).

Research indicates a positive outcome on juries where an intermediary is used: the communication and information elicited from the witness are said to become richer (Collins et al, 2017). The presence of intermediaries has also improved perceptions of interviews with children, with no effect on perceptions of the child (Ridley et al, 2015). There is still a significant gap within the use of intermediaries, and this is seen to have strong links with the ability to conduct thorough assessments and interviews with witnesses and suspects alike (Plotnikoff and Woolfson, 2007; Oxburgh et al, 2016). The term 'intermediary' must not be confused with the term 'appropriate adult': these two roles have different functions and require different levels of qualification. Intermediaries will often be qualified speech and language therapists, able to explain to others how best to communicate with a witness. The appropriate adult role is different, and often they are not qualified to the same level nor can they provide clarity on how best to communicate with a witness during cross-examination.

CROSS-EXAMINATION AND SPECIAL MEASURES

Many people will be familiar with courtroom cross-examination from television portrayals of the often persistent and sometimes intimidating way witnesses will be asked questions in court. In *R v Barker* and *R v T* [1998] 2 NZLR 257 (CA), it was concluded that part of the problem with cross-examination in courts is that it: '*...is seen, wrongly, as an opportunity for advocacy in destroying prosecution witnesses in a zealous and partisan approach which leaves little margin for ethical practice; therefore, affecting those who are vulnerable*' (para.

266). If a case involves a vulnerable or intimidated person, and it is identified that they may need special measures, then this must not be left to chance. The position as set within R v JP [2014] EWCA Crim 2064 was relayed to the court: '...It is now generally accepted that if justice is to be done to the vulnerable witness and also to the accused, a radical departure from the traditional style of advocacy will be necessary. Advocates must adapt to the witness, not the other way round...'. In order for advocates to adapt to the witness, an early assessment, perhaps alongside specialist investigators, will mean that investigators are both inquisitive about people's vulnerabilities and cognisant of the likelihood that the evidence they gather may be used in court. This is important for cross-examination, but the identification of vulnerable and intimidated witnesses must first start with the investigator and within the early stages of the investigation itself.

AVOIDING ASSUMPTION AND ASSESSING WITNESS REQUIREMENTS

It is important that you do not make assumptions about a witness's requirements. There is a legal presumption that all witnesses are competent to give testimony unless information is presented to suggest they are not (YJCEA 1999, s 53). The precise identification method is a key element in addressing the early investigative and later trial needs of witnesses who require special measures; this often goes together with decisions about which evidence should be visually recorded (MoJ, 2011; O'Mahony et al, 2011). Witnesses will often be guided down a particular route depending on, for example, the availability of specially trained officers and the capacity to perform an individual assessment, and the cost to the investigating officers' time (Haber and Haber, 1998; Nield et al, 2003; MoJ, 2011; O'Mahony et al, 2011; McDermott, 2013; Ewin, 2015). This may lead to a decrease in the number of options available to witnesses under the YJCEA in any later trial stage and cause stress to witnesses, so identification of either a vulnerable (YJCEA 1999, s 16) or intimidated (YJCEA 1999, s 17) witness at an early stage in the investigation is key (MoJ, 2011; Doak and McGourlay, 2012). There is a relationship between the methods used to gather evidence, the identification of vulnerable and intimidated witnesses, and later effects on court proceedings (Burton et al, 2006; Bull, 2010; O'Mahony et al, 2011). Burton et al (2006) assert: 'there are large numbers of VIWs, vulnerability is ranged along a spectrum, and needs and wishes need to be ascertained, not assumed' (p 14). The YJCEA does not specifically deal with court familiarisation. However, the law does highlight a difference between familiarisation and special measures: 'There is a difference of substance between the process of familiarisation with the task of giving evidence coherently and the orchestration of evidence to be given. The second is objectionable and the first is not' (R v Salisbury [2005] EWCA Crim 3107: para. 27). One assumption an investigator can make is that certain types of crimes will determine whether special measures are required; however, this assumption is incorrect. Each witness should be assessed on their individual needs, their views should be considered, and a rationale provided about why the evidence has been obtained in any particular way from the witness. The reliability and credibility of the witnesses may also be considered with some caution during the investigation phase.

RELIABILITY AND CREDIBILITY

Terms like reliability and credibility are discussed in the context of witnesses, more often in criminal investigations which are nearing the stage of preparing to charge a suspect with a criminal offence. In some cases, the reliability and credibility of witnesses, and any previous convictions, current circumstances and the way in which their evidence is gathered can influence the investigator's view of their evidence. It is a dangerous and potentially damaging undertaking to assess that a witness is simply not sufficiently credible to give evidence. However, the major factors to consider when determining if a prosecution will be likely include:

- the public interest view of the case;

- the availability and sufficiency of admissible evidence;

- the completeness of the evidence and any undermining material;

- the reliability and credibility of witnesses.

(Wilson, 2008; Doak and McGourlay, 2012; Sprack, 2011; CPS, 2018)

Understanding reliability and credibility is relevant when considering witnesses; however, where this takes place too early, or is based on a subjective view and dependent on poor understandings of criminal law, this can lead to an investigation failing, at least in part due to tunnel vision simply around whether a person should be believed (Doak and McGourlay, 2012; Lea and Lynn, 2012; Sprack, 2011).

Discussing credibility is important in framing discussions about witnesses. It could affect the progression of some cases if a witness is viewed as simply lacking credibility. For example, it was identified within the Rotherham child sexual exploitation and abuse enquiry that the perceived reliability and credibility of witnesses was a problematic feature of the case; this resulted in some early reports not being pursued or taken seriously. This was largely due to the belief that these witnesses, who were mostly vulnerable and intimidated witnesses, were simply not reliable or credible (Jay, 2014, p 74). The position on credibility is outlined in *Onassis v Vergottis* [1968] 2 Lloyds Rep 403 at p 431:

> *Credibility involves wider problems than mere 'demeanour' which is mostly concerned with whether the witness appears to be telling the truth as he now believes it to be... all these problems compendiously are entailed when a Judge assesses the credibility of a witness; they are all part of one judicial process.*

In effect, the issue about the credibility of a witness cannot be considered in isolation from other evidence, or previous character and behaviour.

POLICING SPOTLIGHT

REVISITING THE CASE OF JOHN JONES

A witness may be inherently vulnerable due to some previous, perhaps unscrupulous, behaviour, and while making them vulnerable, it may also mean they are deemed not credible or reliable (*R v Makanjuola* [1995] 3 All ER 730 (CA)). For example, a witness's previous conviction for a dishonesty offence will not make them inherently dishonest. Each witness's circumstances must be judged on the merits of the case and the value of the witness's evidence to the other evidence in the case. Where these occasions are not explored, or are given undue weight too early within an investigation, this can affect the case's overall progression (Jay, 2014; Sprack, 2011). A discourse analysis of criminal case files revealed three dominant speech genres in police and prosecution language: impartiality, credibility and the 'real' victim (Lea and Lynn, 2012). Notions about the value which might be attached to a witness's account of a particular incident could lead investigators to discount important or reasonable lines of enquiry, which may end up further supporting the case, or indeed the witness's version of events. Where this happens, the case can be discontinued if the investigation has been focused too narrowly.

Think about the earlier policing spotlight case of John Jones and consider the following information.

> *John tells the investigators that he has been involved with the police before; they examine his record and find that several years earlier he stole sweets from a shop. The investigators decide that John is not a very honest person and the case against the men who assaulted him is unlikely to succeed.*

The investigators in this case have made a decision about John's credibility, and this has impacted their view of the case. If the investigators were to progress in this way, they would be unlikely to appropriately examine further reasonable lines of enquiry or obtain John's evidence in a fair and thorough way. Remember that demeanour and the past history of a witness's involvement in the criminal justice system, or the simple narrow view of an investigator, are unlikely to be an accurate determination of a witness's credibility. Each witness should have access to justice, especially where they are a victim of crime.

EVIDENCE-BASED POLICING

Research undertaken with the Los Angeles Police Department in 2008 (O'Neal, 2019) revealed that where investigators had beliefs about a victim's character flaws or motives to lie, or where their testimony was inconsistent, or where mental health issues had been identified, they were likely to question the credibility of the witness and the report. The practical implications can be that some crimes are not taken seriously, and some witnesses and victims feel that they have less trust in the police to report future incidents. It is therefore important to examine each case on an induvial basis and refrain from trying to establish whether witnesses are credible or not on the basis of fact-less opinions.

THE CODE OF PRACTICE FOR VICTIMS OF CRIME IN ENGLAND AND WALES

The Victim Code is issued by the Secretary of State for Justice under section 32 of the Domestic Violence, Crime and Victims Act 2004. In November 2020, the Ministry of Justice (2020) set out the 12 rights of victims; this is an important consideration for investigators to comply with the law and also support victims to provide information which might progress a criminal case or following the report of a criminal offence to the police. The rights are as follows.

1. **To be able to understand and to be understood** – this means you must be able to use an interpreter, appropriate adult or intermediary to help communication with the witness. In some cases, this might also mean using sign language for deaf people or using a hearing loop.

2. **To have the details of the crime recorded without unjustified delay** – recording a crime report is a key element to commencing the investigation. This will mean that you will often need the personal details of the person making the report and the location of the incident. This may also mean recording a witness statement or taking a first account.

3. **To be provided with information when reporting the crime** – this could be a letter explaining to the victim the crime reference number and highlighting to them services which are available for support, such as witness care and victim support.

4. **To be referred to services that support victims and have services** – this is a really important step. In order to initiate the right support, you must first understand the victim's needs, and this means asking questions about what might help them.

5. **To be provided with information about compensation** – in some cases compensation through the Criminal Injuries Compensation Scheme might be available; you can check which cases are relevant on the Gov.uk website by searching for victim injury compensation.

6. **To be provided with information about the investigation and prosecution** – arresting a person and charging them might be a small step for the police, but a large stage for victims. This is often the start of proceedings in court, and this can be a daunting time for victims.

7. **To make a Victim Personal Statement** – A Victim Personal Statement is something which tells the court about the impact of the crime on the victim. This is important, especially if a court sentences a defendant, as they will want to hear about what has happened since the victim reported the incident and what has been the impact.

8. **To be given information about the trial, trial process and your role as a witness** – criminal trials can be very daunting and there might be a number of hearings about the case before the witness is needed. Setting expectations about this may help with some of the concerns the witness may have.

9. **To be given information about the outcome of the case and any appeals** – some cases might be concluded, for example if a defendant pleads guilty, without the need for a trial. The outcomes of cases are important and often they might receive a letter from the court. However, it is good practice to advise witnesses and victims about case outcomes.

10. **To be paid expenses and have property returned** – if a victim attends court, they should be paid expenses and if property was seized from them during the investigation then this should be returned as soon as possible once the case has concluded. Returning a victim's or witness's property should be discussed with them to ensure it will not upset, traumatise or embarrass them.

11. **To be given information about the offender following a conviction** – a conviction might be a real point of closure for victims: this is an important step if they are to move on. This information is sometimes communicated to them by the courts, but it is important for victims to receive this information.

12. **To make a complaint about your rights not being met** – a victim may complain to the courts, the police or anybody overseeing police conduct if they believe that their rights have not been met.

CONCLUSION

Witnesses, be they victims or not, should be approached by investigators using an open and diligent approach designed to gain as much detail about what the witness has seen and experienced. If this information later provides support to one hypothesis about the investigation over another, then so be it. However, witnesses are a great source of information to investigators and sometimes this information can be lost, not because of the witness themselves, but because of the approach taken by the investigator. In chapters on interviewing, you will find structured approaches to gathering detail; however, this is not necessarily restricted to suspect interviewing as will be discussed in later chapters. Special Measures, initial accounts, and consideration of intermediaries are all important steps to consider in the management of witnesses. It is critical for investigators to understand, and not assume, a witness's vulnerability. Having spoken to a witness, an investigator should be able to define clearly what they may need in terms of support to get the best evidence from them. A simple acknowledgement that a witness is vulnerable or intimidated may not be enough to legally satisfy the gateways of the YJCEA; a court may challenge an approach to a witnesses evidence if it believes that it is unfair to the legal process for evidence to be admitted in one way over another. Some witnesses who are also victims have additional rights, and these are equally part of the approach to victim and witness management.

These victims' rights are good common-sense actions for any good investigator to follow and are a requirement under the law. If you were to think about being a victim of crime and examine these rights, you would expect that you would be treated fairly, provided with information about the case, and have property returned to you. Maintaining a good relationship with victims is important, especially if they are to have confidence to report future incidents.

SUMMARY OF KEY CONCEPTS

Having read this chapter, you should be able to understand some of the key concepts around dealing with witnesses and victims. This knowledge enables you to:

- understand the processes around obtaining first accounts from witnesses;

- understand the importance of determining if a witness needs support;

- understand the rights around victims according to the Victim Code;

- understand some of the support available under the law for witnesses providing evidence;

- be aware of the roles which might support witnesses, like an intermediary, and their importance to the process of evidence gathering.

CHECK YOUR KNOWLEDGE

1. You are asked to attend reports that someone has witnessed a purse being stolen and the possible suspect has left the scene and the victim is drunk. Are you able to obtain a first account from the drunk victim and what information will you tell them at the scene?

2. What are the differences between section 16 and section 17 of the Youth Justice and Criminal Evidence Act 1999?

3. What are the dangers of judging the value and credibility of a witness too early in the investigation?

Sample answers to these questions are provided at the end of the book.

FURTHER READING

College of Policing (2020) *Authorised Professional Practice: Working with Victims and Witnesses*. [online] Available at: www.app.college.police.uk/app-content/investigations/victims-and-witnesses (accessed 12 November 2021).
Guidance and advice for police officers about working with witnesses.

Crown Prosecution Service (CPS) (2020) *A Guide for Victims & Witnesses*. [online] Available at: www.cps.gov.uk/victims-witnesses (accessed 12 November 2021).
A guide helping to explain court processes and procedures.

Ewin, R (2018) Video Recorded Cross-examination or Re-examination: A Discussion on Practice and Research. *Journal of Applied Psychology and Social Science*, 4(1): 22–38.
A discussion of pre-recorded evidence in criminal trials.

Ellison, L and Munro, V E (2014) A 'Special' Delivery? Exploring the Impact of Screens, Livelinks and Video-recorded Evidence on Mock Juror Deliberation in Rape Trials. Social & Legal Studies, 23(1): 3–29.

Ellison, L and Wheatcroft, J (2010) Could You Ask Me That in a Different Way Please? Criminal Law Review, 11: 823–39.
These are excellent articles for students.

Ministry of Justice (MoJ) (2011) *Achieving Best Evidence in Criminal Proceedings: Guidance on Interviewing Victims and Witnesses, and Guidance on Using Special Measures*. 1st ed. London: Ministry of Justice.
Includes information on the processes around obtaining evidence in more complex cases.

CHAPTER 5
INVESTIGATIVE INTERVIEWING

LEARNING OBJECTIVES

AFTER READING THIS CHAPTER YOU WILL BE ABLE TO:

- design and apply interview plans;
- recognise influences on interviewees' behaviours;
- recognise and implement special warnings and significant statements;
- identify opportunities to introduce bad character evidence.

INTRODUCTION

Omychund v Barker 1744 125 ER establishes the concept of 'best evidence'. In the belief that humans represent the best available evidence to both the investigator and criminal justice system, this chapter will examine interviewing of suspects and witnesses as outlined in Chapter 4 in investigative situations.

Chapter 1 introduced criminal investigation, outlining that an investigation's aim is to discover what happened and who took what part in a criminal event. The investigative interview is a vital part of the process. Interview skills come to the fore in all human interactions, not only in the interview room. Conversations with victims, witnesses and members of the public who may offer insights or intelligence relating to the investigation are vital in obtaining a comprehensive picture, as discussed in Chapter 4.

HISTORICAL DEVELOPMENT OF INVESTIGATIVE INTERVIEWING

Prior to the 1980s, police officers were considered as possessing tacit knowledge of how to conduct investigative interviews. Training was based on observing experienced colleagues. Confessions represented the ultimate aim of the interviewer, and officers obtaining confessions were regarded as the best interviewers.

A combination of high-profile miscarriages of justice, including the Guildford Four (1975), the Birmingham Six (1975) and the Cardiff Three (1988), as well as legislation in the form of the Police and Criminal Evidence Act (PACE) 1984 and the introduction of recorded interviews, gradually removed the veil of secrecy associated with investigative interviews. Against a background of declining public confidence, the 1993 Baldwin report into suspect interviewing practice identified a series of weaknesses centred on meagre preparation, poor technique, a biased approach creating repetitive questions, little attention to detail and an over-reliance on pressurising interviewees. It was apparent that this vital aspect of criminal investigation needed attention. Research into the situation led to the development of the Principles of Investigative Interviewing (covered in detail in the next section) and a national training programme of investigative interviewing (Home Office, 1992). These early examples of research links between police practice and academia resulted in the adoption of the PEACE model of investigative interviewing, which is examined in this chapter.

Police officers engage with a wide variety of people throughout their career. Skills and understanding of interview models will support you in all formal and informal interactions. This chapter follows the professionalisation process, introducing interviewing principles and procedures, legal aspects in the form of the caution, significant statements and silences, special warnings and bad character evidence. Theoretical and practical perspectives provide a richness to your use of this vital investigative skill. This approach is recognised through the provision of investigative principles (Home Office, 1992), which the chapter will start with.

REFLECTIVE PRACTICE 5.1

LEVEL 4

Questioning is a complex skill; you have already spent the majority of your life practising and developing your personal schema, seeking and analysing information. Consider the following.

- When you bought an expensive item, did you ask questions before deciding to purchase it?

- Do you adjust your tone of speech when speaking to young children?

- Have you ever thought of interviewing in investigative drama as bullying?

Did you reflect on why you considered these things important? You have already demonstrated the first steps to a critical understanding of the subject. Now it's time to explore further.

PRINCIPLES OF INVESTIGATIVE INTERVIEWING

As part of the professionalisation of investigative interviewing detailed above, the Home Office (1992) introduced a series of principles, which provide support to your own interviewing practice. The current principles are explained here.

1. The aim of investigative interviewing is to obtain accurate and reliable accounts from victims, witnesses or suspects about matters under police investigation. Probing and questioning an account are vital in gaining a credible account from the interviewee.

2. Investigators must act fairly when questioning victims, witnesses or suspects. They must ensure that they comply with all the provisions and duties under the Equality Act 2010 and the Human Rights Act (HRA) 1998. Article 6 of the HRA outlines our right to a fair trial. The thread of fairness should feature throughout all aspects of a criminal investigation.

3. Investigative interviewing should be approached with an investigative mindset. (Chapter 2 examines the investigative mindset.)

4. Investigators are free to ask a wide range of questions in interviews in order to obtain material which may assist an investigation and provide sufficient evidence or information. Oppressive or repetitive questioning jeopardises the evidential value of the interview; section 76 of PACE details how oppressive or unprofessional conduct may render a confession inadmissible in evidence. The questioning styles section later in this chapter examines this area.

5. Investigators should recognise the positive impact of an early admission in the context of the criminal justice system.

6. Investigators are not bound to accept the first answer given. Questioning is not unfair merely because it is persistent. Avoid allegations of oppression; be confident that a simple reply does not preclude you asking for further detail.

7. Even when a suspect exercises the right to silence, investigators have a responsibility to put questions to them. (The caution and inferences are discussed in this chapter.) Suspects are justified in declining to answer; you are justified in asking questions.

Provided you take an ethical approach to interviewing, knowledge of these principles will support you if called upon to defend your methods. These principles provide a foundation for interviewing. Legal discussion and interview expectations are summarised in the policing spotlight. Following the recommended interview model, as detailed below, is the next step in obtaining a product to be proud of.

POLICING SPOTLIGHT

As an interviewer you will deal with a wide range of people. Some will be used to the criminal justice system and interviewing; for others this will be their only experience. Victims and the public have an expectation that suspect interviewing will be firm and incisive. As a professional it is recognised that you will practise discretion, deciding on the most appropriate approach for the circumstances. The cases of *R v Gowan* 1982 Crim LR rev 821 and *R v Hudson* 72 Crim app 163 (1980) are at first sight contradictory, finding no oppression due to length of interview in Gowan, while a shorter period of questioning was found to be oppressive in Hudson. However, analysis provides the key. Your interviewee is an individual with specific experiences and expectations. Gowan was used to investigative interviews; Hudson was not. You should apply this to your interview planning. A vigorous approach is expected, and your skills in adjusting your approach dependent on your interviewee are as valid in investigations as they are in social discussions.

INTERVIEWING MODELS: PEACE

The mnemonic PEACE refers to the five phases of the investigative interview model arising from research following the 1993 Baldwin report.

- **P**lanning and preparation

- **E**ngage and explain

- **A**ccount, clarification, challenge

- **C**losure

- **E**valuation

Figure 5.1 on page 88 summarises the model. Let's examine each of the elements in turn.

Figure 5.1 PEACE interview elements

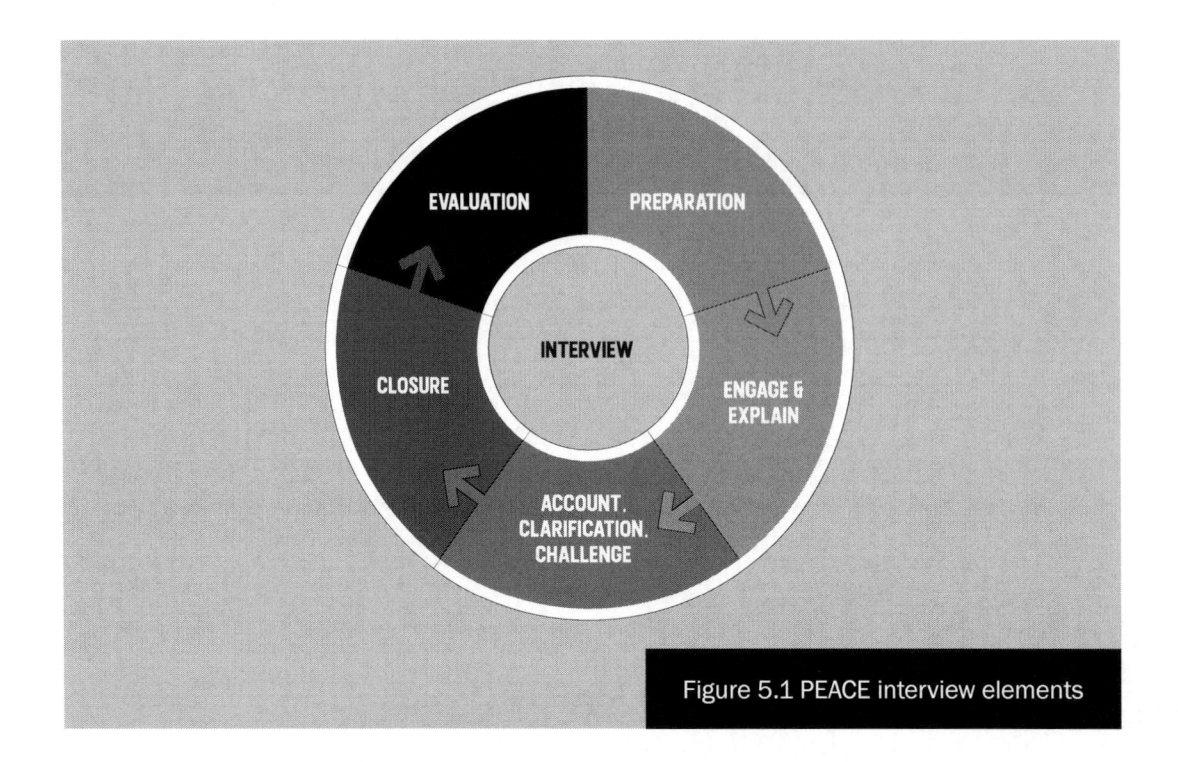

PLANNING AND PREPARATION

Planning and preparation is the element that creates the impression of a 'natural-born interviewer'. Their performance will be a result of planning and preparation rather than an unidentified interviewing gene. Walsh and Milne (2008) found shortfalls in interviews were often linked to poor preparation. To counter this, ensure you have appropriate aims and objectives for the interview you are about to conduct, together with:

- legal knowledge of the offence under investigation, points to prove, significant statements, special warnings and bad character evidence that you intend to use;

- an understanding of the interview model and conversational norms;

- intelligence about your interviewee, community reaction, relationship to the victim, any history of responses to any previous police involvement;

- the context of any allegations;

- your aims and objectives for the interview.

ENGAGE AND EXPLAIN

In our everyday discussions, rapport influences what will follow. This part of the PEACE model includes rapport building. The information should be delivered with this in mind. All our conversations follow a series of rules, as outlined in Schank's (1977) report. Burgess (1984) describes interviews as 'conversations with purpose'. This purposeful element requires the rules to be stated. You are undertaking a criminal investigation; as such, you need to make sure all parties to the conversation are aware of the rules as outlined in the aide-memoire. Encourage the interviewee to contribute fully, without editing their recollection or replies, and to seek clarification where they are unsure of anything. People have a tendency to rely on personal schema or gist memory to fill gaps in their recollection. You can avoid this problematic situation by stressing that it is preferable to concentrate on accurate accounts and memories with the understanding that memories are not chronologically recorded like a recorded film; they are subsequent to a range of influences and consequently may be flawed.

ACCOUNT, CLARIFICATION, CHALLENGE

Conversations are built around topics; imagine speaking with someone about your recent holiday when all their responses were about a work-based event. The flow of conversation would be non-existent and you would probably disengage at the first opportunity. Conversations are dependent upon topics; so are interviews. The interviewer knows that the identification of topics/episodes is vital to the interview. People, places and events are usually specific topics. Arrange your interview to deal with one topic at a time. This maximises the accounts you obtain and assists memory recall by introducing a structure to your 'conversation with purpose'. This is where your listening skills are paramount. Listen to the answers your questions elicit; the interviewee will not be constrained by the topic and nor do you want to discourage their contributions – your role is to assign the material gained to your identified topics. Listening to answers will allow you to probe for detail until you are satisfied that the answers are as accurate and detailed as possible. Where contradictions arise, pause. Obtain the maximum information possible before you start challenging identified contradictions.

CLOSURE

Conversations do not end abruptly. Summarise, allowing the interviewee to correct, alter, add or clarify anything they wish. Signpost what will come next. Do not make promises or predictions.

EVALUATION

Your development as an interviewer is dependent on reflective practice. This follows evaluation of the content of an interview. Have you confirmed or clarified any matters? Identified lines of enquiry? What is the next step following your discovery of this new information?

The PEACE model mirrors conversational styles; you are developing a skill you have spent the majority of your life using. Reflecting on exchanges you have experienced will allow you to develop your own style based on the interviewing model. The next reflective practice activity illustrates how an everyday discussion can be related to the model.

REFLECTIVE PRACTICE 5.2

LEVEL 4

Imagine a social event such as a birthday celebration.

- How did you know when and where to meet your friends, what to wear and how much money to take?

- When you met your friends, was the conversation general?

- When something interesting was mentioned, did you question the explanation?

- As the event came to an end, did you say goodbye to your friends?

- Did you have a good or bad time, and have you shared memories of the event with your friends?

Relate this to the PEACE model. You planned and prepared, engaged, clarified, closed and evaluated the interaction, thereby using each element of the PEACE model. The skills of an interviewer are in your grasp. Reflect on your own conversational style, examining where you can identify links to interview models.

THE CAUTION

The suspect interview starts with the caution; as a policing student you will be familiar with the caution from an early stage of your learning. You are invited to revisit this learning journey in the reflective practice activity. This is an initial and vital part of the suspect interview and it is worth revisiting in detail; if you get this wrong, the whole interview may be ruled inadmissible through sections 76 or 78 of PACE (1984). You will also have created a poor impression of your preparation and professionalism. Conversely, a detailed and accurate approach creates a favourable impression of your capabilities.

This section looks at the caution, significant statements, special warnings and bad character, in a chronological order of consideration, bringing a legal understanding to the interviewer's range of options.

Section 34 of the Criminal Justice and Public Order Act (CJPOA) 1994 qualified a suspect's right to silence, allowing adverse inferences to be drawn in certain circumstances. It is important to note that suspects are entitled to choose silence in answer to questions; however, the suspect who chooses to respond in this manner should be aware that, if the matter results in a prosecution and they advance an explanation or rely on facts they could have reasonably been expected to mention when questioned, the court may draw an adverse inference from the situation.

POLICING SPOTLIGHT

You may be confronted by suspects who choose to exercise their right to silence or reply 'no comment' when interviewed. It is vital that the interviewer continues to ask questions, providing the opportunity for a suspect to answer, treating each question individually. The case of *R v Johnson* [2005] EWCA Crim 971 where a suspect refused to leave their cell to be interviewed confirms that no inference can be drawn from a suspect when questions have not been posed. If the situation had been addressed by questioning the suspect in the cell and they did not mention something they later relied upon, adverse inferences may have been available to the court. Silence in itself is not indicative of guilt. You are able to explain the implications of silence but should not refer to silence in itself being suspicious.

Section 34 of CJPOA sets out the terms to be used when delivering the caution.

> *You do not have to say anything. But, it may harm your defence if you do not mention when questioned something which you later rely on in court. Anything you do say may be given in evidence.*

Code C, Code of Practice to the Police and Criminal Evidence Act (PACE) 1984 outlines that a caution must be given when there are grounds to suspect a person of involvement in an offence before any questions or further questions are put to them. While Code C confirms that minor deviations from the terminology of a caution would not constitute a breach, the failure to caution in exact terms presents a less than professional impression. The interview does not represent a memory test for you: if your preparation would benefit from an aide-memoire or notes, create them. The tone of Code C confirms that a suspect must be aware they are under caution and that they understand the caution and its implications. It is good practice to enquire if a suspect understands the caution after you deliver it. Any reply, positive or negative, is then followed by a request to outline what the interviewee understands. It is recommended this is followed with an explanation in ordinary terms.

In terms of fairness, you will then have met the legal requirements tailored to the needs of the interviewee. The interviewee will have an understanding of the legal implications of the caution to contemplate when deciding on their responses to questions. The legal aspect of adverse inferences continues with special warnings.

REFLECTIVE PRACTICE 5.3

LEVEL 4

The introduction to an investigative suspect interview includes the caution. As a policing student, how much time have you invested in memorising and understanding this legal warning? Contrast your understanding with that of a suspect hearing the caution for the first time, while taking into consideration that you:

- are a policing student;

- have studied 'the caution';

- have access to legal explanations;

- learnt in a calm, measured situation;
- are not experiencing increased stress;
- have prepared.

Replace these suggestions with the following.

- You are suspected of involvement in a criminal offence.
- You are being confronted by an authority figure.
- You are effectively detained; you may be under arrest.
- You are in an unfamiliar environment.
- You are cognitively stressed.
- You are analysing everything that is being said and the likely implications of answers you provide.

How do you think you would perform if examined on the meaning of these 37 words in such an environment? How would it appear to an independent observer if the authority figure did not explain the right to silence and the potential of a court drawing inferences from your questions?

This is why it is good practice to ascertain the interviewee's understanding of the caution.

SIGNIFICANT STATEMENTS

An arrest is a noteworthy event and will often generate a response. PACE recognises this through the significant statement clauses. Arrested persons must not be interviewed about the relevant offences except at a police station (PACE Code C 1.11). If a suspect who has been arrested says something relevant to that offence or another offence, it would be unfair to ignore the comments. Such comments are referred to as 'significant statements'. A significant statement is an unsolicited comment made by the suspect which is relevant to the offence and appears capable of being used in evidence against them, in particular a direct admission of guilt. A significant statement must be a voluntary statement, not one made in reply to a question. That would amount to an interview as defined by Code C of PACE. A significant statement or silence is something which appears capable of being used in evidence, in particular a direct admission of guilt. A failure or refusal to answer a question or to answer it satisfactorily which may give rise to an inference may amount to a significant silence. A significant statement can arise at any time, but a significant silence can only arise after the caution. (The policing spotlight illustrates how a significant statement may occur in a real-world example.) You must make a written record of any comments made by a suspect, including unsolicited comments, which are outside the context of an interview but which might be relevant to the offence. The written record must be timed and signed by the maker. When practicable, the suspect shall be given the opportunity to read that record and to sign it as correct or to indicate how they consider it inaccurate. PACE Code E 4.3b states '*At the beginning of an interview at a Police Station, following caution, Interviewing Officers shall put to the suspect any significant statement or silence which occurred prior to the interview and shall invite the suspect to confirm or deny the earlier statement or silence*'. This meets the legal requirements, and questions based on the content of the significant statement or silence should be planned into the appropriate interview topic.

POLICING SPOTLIGHT

A person was arrested on suspicion of a series of robberies throughout the north of England. Without prompting, they voluntarily claimed they had been at a separate location at the time of one of the offences; they continued to elaborate giving precise details of what was suspected to be the foundations of an alibi. The comments were noted and introduced into evidence as significant statements. Enquiries proved the claims to be false, proving the arrested person had provided a series of false claims.

SPECIAL WARNINGS

Sections 36 and 37 of the Criminal Justice and Public Order Act (CJPOA) outline circumstances when a court may be asked to draw an inference in relation to specific acts. Comparison with the section 34 caution highlights that, under section 34 an adverse inference may be drawn if a suspect presents new information at court where it could have been reasonably expected to be presented at interview. In the case of sections 36 and 37, if a suspect fails to explain a relevant issue at interview, an adverse inference may later be drawn at court with no requirement for 'new information'.

SECTION 36

A suspect is arrested and there is found on their person, or in their clothing or footwear, or otherwise in their possession, or in the place where they were arrested, any objects, marks or substances, or marks on such objects, and the person fails or refuses to account for the object's marks or substances found. A court or jury may draw a proper inference from this silence.

SECTION 37

An arrested person is found and arrested by a constable at a place at or about the time the offence for which they were arrested was committed; the person fails or refuses to account for their presence at that place. A court or jury may be asked to draw an inference from that silence.

Section 36 warnings apply in respect of objects, marks or substances or marks on objects, for example, items found in pockets, bloodstains on the person, clothing or objects, bruising and scarring. Should the suspect fail to account for this to the officer's satisfaction, a special warning may be given. Section 37 extends this to address their presence at a particular place at a particular time.

A special warning can only be given if the person fails or refuses to account for specific matters: it follows that questions must be asked to ascertain that they are failing or refusing to account for these matters; a special warning is indeed a challenge and should be incorporated into this part of the interview. The special warning must include the following five points, presented in a style understandable to the interviewee.

1. Nature of the offence being investigated.

2. The fact the suspect is being asked to account for.

3. That the officer believes the fact exists due to the suspect's involvement in the offence.

4. That an inference may be drawn if the suspect fails to account for the fact.

5. That a record of the interview is being made.

It is important that the suspect is given the opportunity to respond to the warning, normally by the original question being repeated.

> ## CRITICAL THINKING ACTIVITY 5.1
>
> ### LEVEL 6
>
> Sections 36 and 37 of the CJPOA allow adverse inferences to be drawn where a suspect fails or refuses to account for specific matters. The legislation requires the person to have been arrested. Critically evaluate whether the requirement to have this suspicion will influence your view as to what constitutes a satisfactory account.

BAD CHARACTER EVIDENCE

The murder of eight-year-old Sarah Payne by convicted sex offender Roy Whiting in 2000 is associated with two significant legal developments. A campaign by her mother Sara Payne led to the introduction of the Child Sex Offenders Disclosure Scheme (Sarah's Law). It was widely reported that the revelations of Whiting's previous offending following his conviction influenced the then Home Secretary, David Blunkett, in introducing bad character evidence through the Criminal Justice Act (CJA) 2003. This introduced a suspect's previous offending or history of reprehensible behaviours. Prior to the 2003 act, previous findings of guilt could be introduced through a range of doctrines and legislation in a confusing environment. CJA effectively simplified the legality of similar fact evidence. If you identify and intend to introduce such evidence to the interview, you should familiarise yourself with the legal position. In line with the preparation element of PEACE, this is an important part of maintaining a professional impression.

Section 98 of the CJA explains that bad character refers to evidence of, or a disposition towards, misconduct in connection with the offence in question. This may take the form of previous convictions or 'a disposition towards misconduct'. Preparation is key to discovering convictions or behaviours which may amount to bad character evidence. Such material can only be introduced to the interview if the interviewer is aware of the detail.

Previous convictions are self-explanatory. 'Misconduct' is defined as 'reprehensible' or other behaviour which in the view of an objective, reasonable person would be disapproved of, such as anti-social behaviour or lying. This broadens the range of behaviours which may be regarded as providing evidence of bad character. Bad character evidence is only admissible if:

- it is of important explanatory value in that a court or jury would be unable to understand the situation without reference to it;

- it is of substantive probative value in relation to the matter in issue;

- it is of substantial importance to the case as a whole;

- all parties agree to its admissibility. This is unlikely in an interview situation.

If the evidence of misconduct falls within the definition of bad character, it can be admitted if one or more of the 'gateways' apply.

1. All parties agree. This is unlikely in an interview situation. Should this arise you are advised to seek legal guidance.

2. Adduced by the defendant or given in answer to a question. Iain Stainton has experienced defendants referring to their own bad character at interview, for example: 'You know my past. I only break into shops not people's houses'.

3. Important explanatory evidence. This is an important gateway where, without referring to a history containing bad character, a court or jury would be unable to understand other evidence. For example, a witness refers to identifying a person they only know from their previous offending.

4. Relevant to an important matter in issue between the defendant and prosecution. This addresses a propensity or tendency to commit a type of offence or to be untruthful. A variety of offences under the Theft Act 1968 and 1978 and the Sexual Offences Act 2003 as categorised by Statutory Instrument (S.I.) 2004 No 3346 as indicative of a propensity to commit other offences are covered in the Bad Character provisions of Part 11, chapter 1 of the Criminal Justice Act 2003. Any other offence may be considered as demonstrating a propensity if a link can be shown. For example, a conviction for possessing a bladed article may indicate a propensity to commit robbery if the method was linked to a bladed article.

5. Substantial probative value to an important matter between the defendant and a co-defendant. This applies where a defendant argues their co-defendant committed an offence because of their offending history.

6. To correct a false impression given by the defendant. Where a defendant attempts to create a false impression of themselves, this may be corrected by reference to past behaviours or convictions.

7. Where the defendant attacks another person's character. The corrective theme allows attacks on others' characters to be addressed by reference to the defendant's character.

When interviewing you should plan to use bad character evidence, firstly by discovering the material and then by recognising when a gateway occurs. The issue of an individual's propensity to behave in a certain manner is a relevant part of the investigative process; as such these matters should form part of an interview plan. If the evidence is that of a propensity to be untruthful, how can this be proved? Offences under the Fraud Act 2006 are likely to contain elements of untruthfulness. A history of findings of guilt following not guilty pleas are indicative of untruthfulness. A person can be dishonest without being untruthful!

Evidence of bad character is without doubt a challenge that usually features in the later sections of policing courses. Deal with matters relevant to the offence within the first phase of your challenge. This can then be followed by bad character, providing a legitimate gateway has been identified. The introduction of bad character evidence is best scheduled at the end or even in a separate later interview. Bad character is not first-hand evidence of the commission of an offence; it is supportive of behaviours and will not replace missing probative evidence.

QUESTIONING STYLES

The phrase 'investigative interviewing' emphasises the collaborative nature of contemporary interviewing that would not occur in an 'interrogation'. The information you gather will be a direct result of the questions you pose. Where a suspect is being untruthful, they are cognitively stressed; creating lies the interviewer will accept is challenging in itself. Remembering what they have already answered and the accounts given is a difficult process. As outlined in the policing spotlight, your questioning is expected to be vigorous but fair. Loftus and Palmer's seminal (1974) experiment highlights how the interviewer's language influences the answers given. Their use of leading questions distorted the interviewee's memory, leading to false claims. In courtroom dramas you will have heard claims of 'leading question' raised as a legal representative raises their concerns as to its fairness. Leading questions are created when the interviewer introduces material that undermines the credibility and accuracy of answers given.

The interviewer opens an interview, whether with a witness or suspect, by encouraging the interviewee to provide the maximum amount of information. The response to your initial question sets the parameters: for example, 'tell me what happened from lunchtime until the point of your arrest'. The maxim of quantity suggests people respond with the amount of information they feel is required and no more. Baker's (1907) 12 Golden Rules of Conversation emphasises the maxim through rule one, 'avoid unnecessary detail': this rule of everyday conversation is unlikely to be applicable in an investigative interview. Repetitive questioning does not produce a collaborative atmosphere and may be viewed as oppressive. Asking an interviewee to 'tell', 'explain' and 'describe' (TED) is a conversational style, where the other party is asked to address the same question several times, with each one producing more information as the maxim evolves. You can introduce elements of precision by adding 'precisely', 'in detail' and 'exactly' (PIE) to the questions. The TED PIE mnemonic represents one of the most effective ways of opening any conversation. Follow the open theme with who, what, when, where, why and how questions (5WH) as you probe the detail. Gaps in the story will remain even from the most helpful interviewee, so closed and option questions are an acceptable way of filling gaps as you funnel the information (Figure 5.2) gained from general to specific.

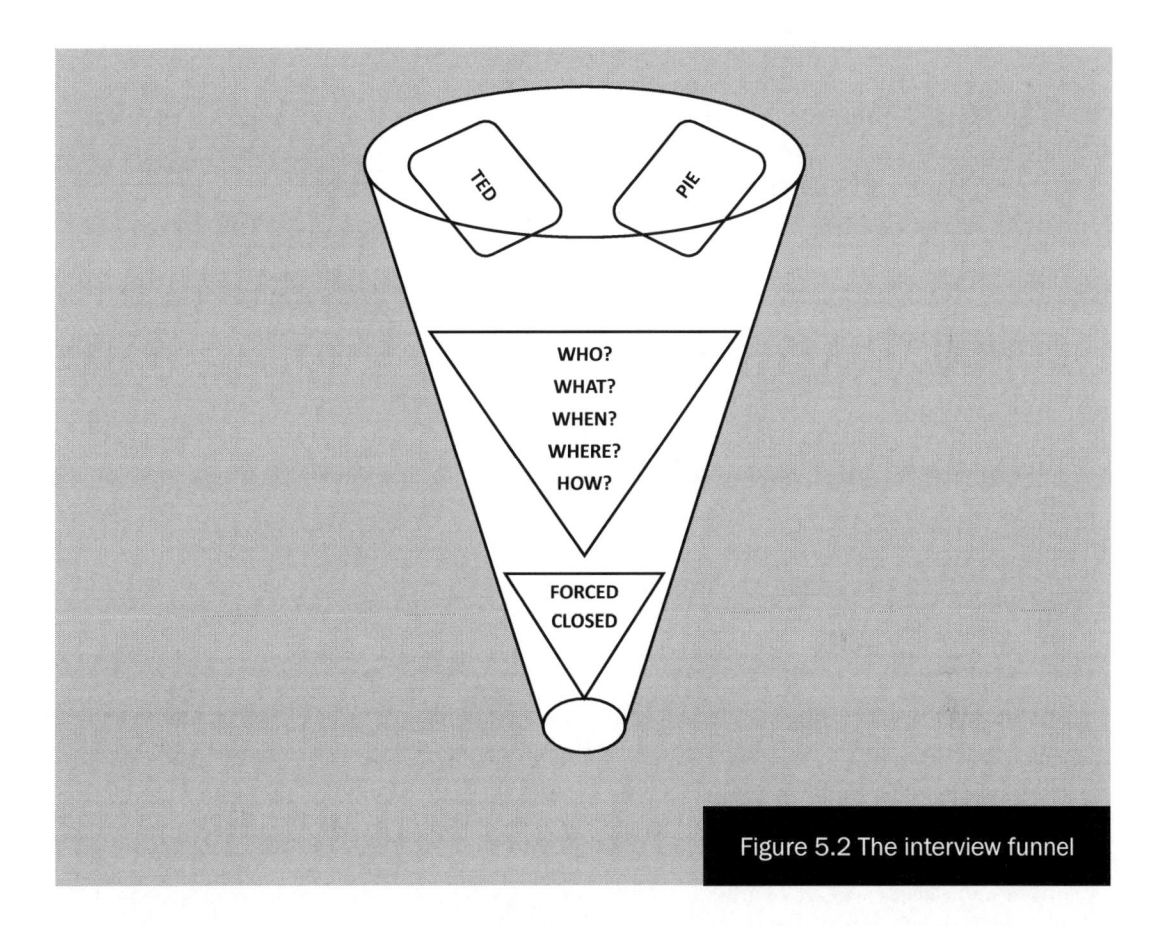

Figure 5.2 The interview funnel

The interviewer must be professional; formality does not necessarily equal professionalism. Consider the situation outlined in the reflective practice activity and be yourself in style. Consider the impression you would take from the situations in the reflective practice activity. The ideal option for a senior investigating officer (SIO) is having a cachet of professional interviewers who bring their differing personalities and approaches to the same interview model. This allows the SIO to choose the best options for particular interviews.

> **REFLECTIVE PRACTICE 5.4**
>
> **LEVEL 4**
>
> You are a policing student reading this chapter on investigative interviewing. You have also been exposed to a lifetime of crime fiction where aggressive, interrupting questioning is often the norm. Consider identified miscarriages of justice such as the Birmingham Six or Cardiff Three. Then compare the interview practices you have identified to those outlined here, which will allow you to draw a conclusion as to the preferable approach for the professional interviewer.

CONDUCTING THE INTERVIEW

This section will introduce the conversation management model of interviewing (Shepherd and Griffiths, 2013), showing you how to begin, develop and challenge in an interview setting.

INTRODUCTION

Introducing the interview is a constant element since legal matters such as the caution and significant statements, previously introduced in this chapter, rarely vary. You will have heard about the importance of first impressions; the introduction is the first opportunity to make that impression confident and professional. Figure 5.3 highlights how the interview should progress.

Start the questioning phase of the interview with a first account. This is where you pose open questions based on the TED PIE approach referred to above. This will encourage the interviewee to expand on their initial response, recognising you are seeking expansive answers and tailor their responses accordingly. The information you gain will give you an impression of the interviewee's likely responses and their acceptance of any allegations or otherwise. Summaries are important throughout the interview: demonstrating your listening skills and confirming information given while allowing for corrections and clarifications. Summarise the first account before moving on to your initial topic.

Interview process

- Open question to establish detailed information → **First account**
- Plan still relevant? Choose topic to develop → **Review**
- Open question to expand topic → **Open topic**
- Question to gather detailed information → **Probe**
- Check understanding, clarify material provided → **Summary**
- Use evidence, discrepancies in account → **Challenge**
- **Link**

Figure 5.3 Interview process

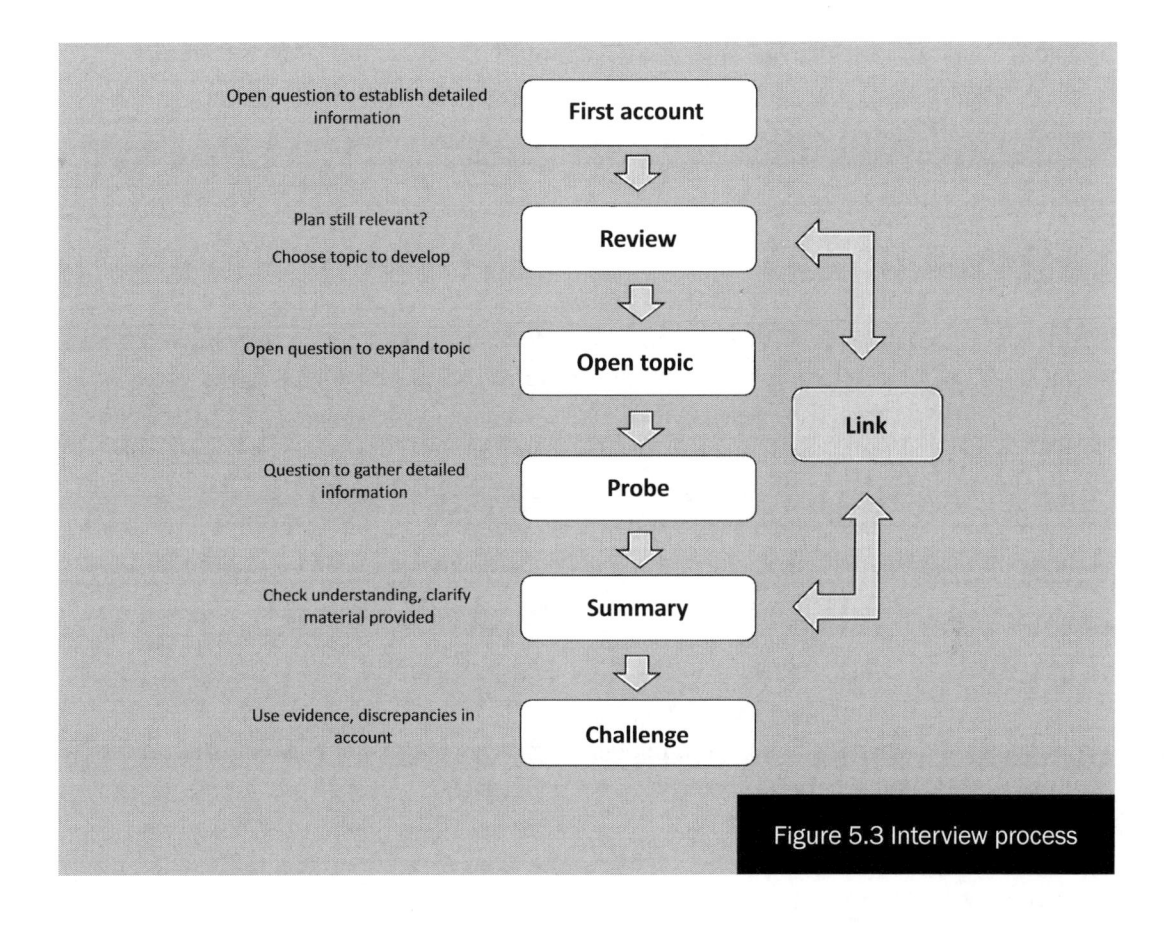

TOPICS

You already use topics in your conversations. For example, if you are discussing a recent holiday and the other party to the conversation replies about their love of chocolate, further discussion would be difficult; if, however, they reply about their holiday experience then the conversation will likely develop along that theme. Further topics, such as a place you visited or event you attended on the holiday, will naturally form further topics. Identifying and utilising topics within the investigative interview provides a structure to maximise your information gathering, aiding memory retrieval by concentrating on specific aspects. People, places and events will generally be topics in an interview. You are able to identify likely topics by assessing your information of the offence. Topics may alter as a result of the interviewee's responses. Address each topic in the funnel questioning style noted earlier (see Figure 5.2), remembering to summarise before moving to the next topic. Advance through your topics chronologically. Where contradictions occur, probe the answers given; do not challenge at this stage. When you are satisfied you have obtained the maximum amount of information about the topic, summarise and move on.

PROBING

The aim is to obtain full, truthful accounts that will withstand scrutiny. As the interviewer you are the initial scrutineer, and it is important to use the probing stage to establish facts, not for challenging the account provided. When probing reveals continuing anomalies and contradictions with other material supplied or other investigative material, these should be challenged at the appropriate stage. Schedule your challenges after the maximum amount of material and explanation has been obtained through the topics stage. Alternative explanations should not be an option for the interviewee in the challenge stage of the interview. Interviewees have a right not to reply although PACE Code C 10:10 confirms that failure or refusal to answer or to answer satisfactorily may lead to the court drawing an inference, as outlined in the caution section above. Oppressive interviews may be ruled inadmissible under the terms of section 78 of PACE. A court may dismiss a confession if it appears to have been obtained by oppression or any other behaviour rendering it unreliable (PACE, s 76). The next policing spotlight outlines legal guidance and expectations of the interview. Remember a court will view the interview as a whole, and that confessions are not the ultimate aim. Do not pursue your challenges beyond what is reasonable. You may find it frustrating that an interviewee does not confess when confronted with what you believe to be ideal evidence. The court may also view the interview like this. Repetitive, bullying challenges are unacceptable in a professional criminal investigation environment. Make your point, probe it and move on. Figure 5.3 suggests a process to be followed in structuring your interview.

CHALLENGES

Figure 5.3 accentuates the place for challenges. When you have obtained all the explanations and information available through questioning and probing, it is time to move to challenges. You may feel it wise to take a short break to formulate challenges identified during the interview or move straight into this phase; both are acceptable. Your knowledge of the case material will allow you to frame challenges where the accounts provided contradict or do not withstand scrutiny. Construct your challenges from minor to major, scaffolding in importance. Remain objective, give the interviewee the chance to reply and listen to their answers, which may require further probing. Do not become involved in an argument even when you cannot see any benefit to continued denials. You can emphasise your challenges vigorously without being oppressive. Special warnings and bad character should feature in this part of the interview and can be planned in advance. When you and the interviewee have nothing further to add, conclude the interview.

CRITICAL THINKING ACTIVITY 5.2

LEVEL 5

Shepherd and Griffiths (2013) discuss how conversational behaviours contribute to establishing a rapport between the interviewer and interviewee, emphasising the contribution empathy can make. In contrast, Oxburgh et al (2012) found no evidence to support the claim that the use of empathy leads to an increased amount of relevant information being obtained during an interview.

Contrast these findings alongside your own experience in deciding whether time spent on establishing rapport in the interview is worthwhile.

CONCLUSION

Interview models are based on skills you have developed from an early age. Conversational skills are embedded in all our social interactions. Investigative interviewing brings a structure to these lifelong skills, creating a 'conversation with purpose'. Contemporary techniques such as deoxyribonucleic acid (DNA) analysis, and CCTV and communications data scrutiny are valuable. However, they will not solve crimes without support. They may place an individual at a location but are unlikely to explain why. The eyewitness may be able to rely on their five senses to supplement their account. Humans bring context, opinion and suggestion to the investigation. Some may be evidential, others merely informative; all will have value in creating a comprehensive picture. PACE and the introduction of audio-recorded interviews created a revolution in professionalising investigative interviewing. As interviews continue to transition to video and audio recording, will this drive further developments?

This chapter introduced the investigative practice of interviewing both the suspect and witnesses. Legal requirements such as the caution have been outlined, while significant statements and special warnings were included to assist your interviewing practice. Bad character evidence was explained in sufficient detail for you to include this in your interviewing practice. The chapter content will help you develop your own interview practice; be aware that this often results in you commenting on interview practice in crime dramas!

SUMMARY OF KEY CONCEPTS

This chapter has introduced investigative interviewing, outlining the importance of gaining truthful, accurate accounts from both suspects and witnesses. The content enables you to:

- prepare and conduct interviews;
- choose a questioning style to complement the situation;
- administer 'the caution' lawfully and professionally;
- recognise and utilise significant statements;
- employ special warnings in an interview scenario;
- interpret the law relating to bad character evidence;
- design interview strategies for a range of suspect and witness situations.

CHECK YOUR KNOWLEDGE

1. You are preparing to interview a detained person on suspicion of theft. The circumstances are that officers attended a burglar alarm at a local builders' merchants; on their arrival a person was seen to run away. Enquiries led to the detained person being arrested. An inexperienced colleague asks if you will be

issuing a section 37 Criminal Justice and Public Order Act 1994 Special Warning. Reply to your colleague with justifications for your choice.

2. You are conducting enquiries with customers in a local pub following an assault. You approach a group with a view to asking if they had witnessed anything. One of the group steps forward asking you 'Who says it was me? They have no idea'. A colleague makes you aware this person fits a distinctive description of the offender. You arrest and caution the person. You would like to refer to their comment at interview but are unsure if comments made before a caution can be used. A colleague suggests this may be a 'significant statement'. Are they correct? Outline how you would introduce the comment to the interview?

3. You are conducting an interview with a colleague where the suspect responds 'no comment' to the questions posed. Your colleague seems frustrated, seeing little point in continuing the interview in such circumstances. You decide to take a short break in the interview. Summarise your interview plan to your colleague.

4. Complete the blanks.

T

....

Explain

D

....

Precisely

I

....

Exactly

Sample answers to these questions are provided at the end of the book.

FURTHER READING

The College of Policing Authorised Professional Practice (APP) web pages provide a searchable resource, covering many aspects of policing, including investigative interviewing. The guidance can be found here: www.app.college.police.uk/

Fisher, R and Geiselman, R E (1992) *Memory Enhancing Techniques for Investigative Interviewing: The Cognitive Interview*. Springfield, IL: Charles C Thomas.
This book explores the origins of cognitive interviewing.

Gudjonsson, G H (2018) *The Psychology of False Confessions: Forty Years of Science and Practice*. Hoboken, NJ: Wiley.
The author writes extensively about interviewing. This book brings the history of interview research up to date.

Milne, R and Roberts, K (2011) *Investigative Interviewing*. Bingley: Emerald.
These authors have worked with practitioners for many years. This book examines the application of theory in practical environments.

Shepherd, E and Griffiths, A (2013) *Investigative Interviewing: The Conversation Management Approach*. 2nd ed. Oxford: Oxford University Press.
A comprehensive book explaining interviewing in detail.

CHAPTER 6
SPECIALIST SUPPORT

LEARNING OBJECTIVES

AFTER READING THIS CHAPTER YOU WILL BE ABLE TO:

- choose specialist contributors to your investigations;
- prepare case papers to support expert analysis;
- combine with other agencies to the benefit of your investigations;
- explain evidential requirements for expert opinion.

INTRODUCTION

Chapter 1 inspected the evolution of the investigator, drawing on historic perceptions of the expert dispatched to help investigations into serious crimes. You will have realised that this depiction of criminal investigation is not entirely accurate. Investigative actions may help you to accumulate an eclectic array of material; however, the skill in interpreting this is dependent upon drawing on a range of knowledge and experience. From crime scene investigators to communication experts, the proficient investigator knows how to draw upon these specialisms and manage their contributions to the investigation. This chapter will introduce specialist support options available. Search advisors, financial investigators and communication data specialists all provide valuable support to you as an investigator. Specialists in the fields of social media, body-worn videos, profiling and biometrics will help you utilise the material these specialisations can provide. Policing cannot operate remotely from other agencies; this is particularly relevant to investigations where a multi-agency approach is often required. Drawing on the services of subject experts requires knowledge of how to introduce their opinions as evidence, all of which will be discussed in this chapter.

ORIGINS OF EXPERTS

Fingerprint analysis is one of the best-known contributors to the specialist investigative armoury. Sir Francis Galton published his book outlining how the unique characteristics of fingerprints could be used to identify individuals in 1892, coinciding with the first recorded use of fingerprints in a criminal investigation – the 1892 Rojas murder in Argentina where fingerprint analysis contributed to the prosecution of a mother for the murder of her two sons. The first recorded use of fingerprints in a criminal investigation in the UK did not occur until the 1902 conviction of Henry Jackson for burglary at a snooker hall, where his fingerprints were recovered from the scene. Fingerprint analysis demonstrates how specialists can contribute from the earliest stages of an investigation through their work at a crime scene to the culmination where expert evidence is provided to a court. Suitable qualified fingerprint specialists are regarded as experts by the criminal justice system, an important factor which will be explored shortly.

SEARCH ADVISORS

Searches feature throughout investigations: from crime scenes to searches following arrest, from searching people to vast areas, the stories that can be told through searching are many and varied. The conduct of a search is a specialised skill in itself. Police Search Advisors (POLSA) are proficient in all types of search and can often be found in major enquiries advising and managing searches.

Some of the most urgent types of search involve missing people, and the management of these is of paramount importance, particularly where public appeals result in volunteers. Without proper control it would soon become impossible to know what areas had been searched and to what extent, hindering rather than assisting an enquiry. Operation Fincham, the 2002 investigation into the deaths of Holly Wells and Jessica Chapman, attracted criticism for the lack of preparedness the investigative team put into place to deal with the public response that two young girls were missing. The following policing spotlight illustrates how specialisms combine with traditional practice to produce results.

POLICING SPOTLIGHT

During an investigation into the supply of controlled drugs, it became apparent that the suppliers had developed a method of concealing drug stashes in remote areas of the countryside. The terrain precluded any form of surveillance where the exact locations could be identified. Liaison with forensic archaeologists introduced the investigative team to the principle of Winthroping (Hunter and Cox, 2005). This method of analysing the landscape and identifying prominent features arose from counter-terrorism operations and has been used to identify deposition sites for human remains. An expert in the practice was engaged and provided with as much detail as possible about the general areas suspected of being used. With their assistance, a series of drug stashes were identified, enabling further forensic opportunities and focused human and technical surveillance to be deployed. This combination of tactics was dependent upon understanding and following the expert advice, confirming that no single element solves crime, but one element may be the key to unlocking a series of techniques which do.

CRITICAL THINKING ACTIVITY 6.1

LEVEL 5

Crime scenes can tell a variety of stories. Profilers, communication data specialists and experts in a wide variety of subjects, including forensic archaeologists, fire service specialists, river and tide patterns, to name a few, can all contribute information and the hypothesis they produce from the crime scene.

As an investigator, summarise what information or material you can gain from analysing a crime scene to complement forensic examination.

FINANCIAL INVESTIGATORS

Motivation to commit crime often arises from the acquisition of money. The importance of financial investigation is recognised by legislation: the Proceeds of Crime Act 2002 is designed to counter criminally obtained assets and money laundering. This specialised area of investigation should be considered in either intelligence-led or reactive investigations where you identify a financial aspect as well as the more commonly encountered seizure and retrieval of criminally acquired assets, often at the conclusion of a prosecution. Consider how much your financial activities and background says about you and then translate that to criminality, where the criminal may be trying to disguise their criminal profit through money laundering. Financial investigation is appropriate for intelligence gathering and reactive investigations. Prosecution is sometimes seen as the end of an investigation (see Chapter 9), and financial investigation can complement your investigation by following criminal assets with a view to retrieving them from offenders.

REFLECTIVE PRACTICE 6.1

LEVEL 4

It is likely that you have a credit or debit card and telephone handset in easy reach right now. Take a moment to deliberate how you have used these two items in the past few days.

- What have you paid for?

- Have you added funds, and if so where from?

- Who have you communicated with?

- What internet sites have you visited?

- What photographs have you taken and stored?

Now imagine what a suspect would be doing with similar items. Consider how the respective specialist could help you to assemble the metaphorical jigsaw referred to throughout this book.

COMMUNICATIONS DATA

The value of data to investigations is wide and varied; from missing persons to organised crime, the contribution of digital data is significant. This section will concentrate on phone data, which is available in two main forms: that created by using the device and the data contained on the device.

The UK government describe communications data as the who, where, when and how of communications (Home Office, 2015). The content of a communication is a highly specialised area that this book does not have the space to explore.

In the digital environment, data is created in a number of ways, including:

- call data;
- social network use;
- location services;
- travel records;
- wearables;
- financial transactions;
- loyalty schemes;

- ID cards;
- access cards;
- IP addresses;
- email;
- WiFi;
- Bluetooth.

The acquisition of communications data from usage is governed by the Regulation of Investigatory Powers Act 2000 and the Investigatory Powers Act 2016. As explained in Chapter 7, the necessity and proportionality of your investigative requirements are central to any requests. Subject to correct authorisation, communications service providers can provide information on phone usage, such as:

- subscriber details;
- outgoing calls;
- incoming calls;
- senders and recipients of SMS;

- location;
- financial records;
- diverts.

Extracting data from a lawfully obtained handset can provide:

- SMS content;
- internet-centred messaging content;
- notes pages;
- contact lists;
- pictures, video, audio;
- calendar entries.

While the majority of us are familiar with operating mobile devices, it is unlikely you are qualified to probe handsets to an evidential standard. With this in mind, the Association of Chief Police Officers (now National Police Chiefs Council) (2012b) introduced the following principles for digital evidence.

1. That no action is taken that should change data held on a digital device including a computer or mobile phone that may subsequently be relied upon as evidence in court.

2. Where a person finds it necessary to access original data held on a digital device that the person must be competent to do so and able to explain their actions and the implications of those actions on the digital evidence to a court.

3. That a trail or record of all actions taken that have been applied to the digital evidence should be created and preserved. An independent third-party forensic expert should be able to examine those processes and reach the same conclusion.

4. That the individual in charge of the investigation has overall responsibility to ensure that these principles are followed.

Despite their age in this constantly developing environment, these principles continue to provide core foundations for this area of investigation. You will require digital information in your role as an investigator, and the information you seek should be precise, necessary and proportionate in nature. You cannot trawl through devices in the hope of gaining information without good reason (see the case of Allen, Chapter 9). Take note of your local policies for referring devices on for expert analysis and the information you gain will meet evidential requirements. The case of *R v E* [2018] confirms the guidance that mobile phones should not be examined as a matter of course; the decision to examine should be based on a specific identified requirement to do so.

POLICING SPOTLIGHT

Imagine yourself in the position of lead investigator in a missing person enquiry. A person has been reported missing and their actions have led to concern for their safety. Enquiries reveal they have travelled to a large rural county in their car. Serious welfare concerns allow you to access communications cell site data, which confirms their device is in a particular area. Owing to the rural nature this is a significant expanse. Little CCTV or automatic number plate recognition (ANPR) is available.

Communicating this information with the family reveals a favourite place of the missing person to be within the area. You direct colleagues in a focused search based on this information, finding the missing person who was preparing to harm themselves. This description based on an actual event shows how, when no single element will provide a result, combining them will.

SOCIAL MEDIA

Social media represents a hitherto non-existent public space, and as with any emerging environment, norms and rules need to develop. Parameters are created from practice and experience. The origins of intelligence are valid but pose the risk of analogue approaches being unsuited for a digital world when not considered in context.

Social media intelligence may consist of specific personal material harvested from a social media environment or the broader church of community intelligence. Community intelligence is defined by Her Majesty's Inspectorate of Constabulary, Fire and Rescue Services as:

> *Local information, direct or indirect, that when assessed provides intelligence on the quality of life experienced by individuals and groups, that informs both the strategic and operational perspectives in the policing of communities.*
>
> (HMICFRS, 2001, p 35)

Lawful monitoring of the public place of social media is acceptable and often referred to as 'open source', sitting in plain sight. Monitoring this public space to gain context and information about forthcoming or past events can be considered good policing. Overt monitoring and engagement can be seen as traditional lines of enquiry in a new environment. Introducing a covertness to your engagement propels your action into the realms of the 2000 Regulation of Investigatory Powers Act (RIPA), particularly surveillance, or covert human intelligence sources (CHISs). If your proposed enquiries are likely to involve such actions, refer to your local RIPA officers. Some basic guidance can be found in Chapter 7.

The investigative opportunities to be found in the wider digital environment are many and varied, and this book does not have the space to explore the worldwide web, internet-enabled devices, information available from commercial sources or the internet of things. The College of Policing's Authorised Professional Practice pages remain in development at the time of writing, and you should speak with your force specialist who will be able to advise.

FACIAL BIOMETRICS

Chapter 2 refers to the investigative benefits of tracing CCTV material. Contemporary developments see CCTV harnessing facial recognition capabilities. While CCTV is part of mainstream investigative practice, facial biometrics currently sit within specialist fields.

The first CCTV contribution to criminal investigation occurred in 1933 when Robert Norbury created the first security camera to help him solve the following dilemma: who is stealing eggs from my chicken coup? The British Security Industry Association (2020) estimates there are currently in the region of 6 million active cameras in the UK, of which 11,000 are automatic number plate recognition (ANPR) (Police.UK, 2021). Significant expansion and the origins of ANPR can be traced to the IRA bombing campaign of the early 1990s. Facial recognition technology was first trialled in the UK by Newham council in 1998 when a series of cameras were linked to police photographic databases with the aim of flagging if and when prolific offenders entered the city centre; as remains common, this requires an interface between the technology and human operators to provide a full picture. The trial did not lead to any arrests but a 34 per cent decrease in robberies, which can be attributed to the deterrent effect (Parliamentary Office of Science and Technology 2001).

Facial biometrics can be sub-divided into three sections addressing:

1. identification;

2. authentication;

3. retrospective.

An example of identification and authentication is the unlocking technology found in many mobile devices where the user is identified, which in turn provides authority for continuing use. Retrospective use refers to identifying unknown suspects from CCTV or similar images obtained during an investigation. This type of identification must take place in line with Code D of the Police and Criminal Evidence Act 1984. The Metropolitan Police deployed overt facial recognition technology when policing the Notting Hill Carnival in 2016; an alert system notified officers when persons of interest were detected, confirming the on-going requirement for systems to interface with officers themselves. Similar trials conducted by South Wales Police led to the case *R (Bridges) v Chief Constable of South Wales Police and Ors* [2020], which has ramifications for facial recognition practice within law enforcement.

The case was brought by Edward Bridges, a civil liberties campaigner from Cardiff, concerning the lawfulness of the facial recognition techniques deployed by South Wales Police on a number of occasions between 2017 and 2019. The technique screened images against a 'watchlist' of wanted persons, with any positive identifications being passed to an operator for further action. The claim was that the technology was incompatible with Article 8 of the Human Rights Act 1998, the Equality Act 2010 and data protection law. The original claim was dismissed, leading to an appeal which found that the interference with Mr Bridge's privacy was unlawful, as were the equality considerations. In a reflection of the origins of the Regulation of Investigatory Power Act 2000 (described in Chapter 7), the court found that the guidance and legal framework to support the tactic was lacking, becoming over reliant on officers' individual discretion. Collateral intrusion (Chapter 7) was a further concern, as was the effectiveness of the technology in race and gender bias. The court recommended that this be examined, and measures introduced to address it. This does not necessarily make facial recognition unlawful, but does confirm the requirement for a precise legal framework to support its application.

BODY-WORN VIDEO

Body-worn video (BWV) are overt video and audio recording devices commonly worn on officers' chests. It is inappropriate and impractical to constantly record so devices are activated by the officer in accordance with their force's policy. Footage is uploaded to a force database as soon as practicable. Practitioners should take into account collateral intrusion issues, as defined in Chapter 7. BWV provides the option to record events that officers take part in, supplementing conventional statements, the overt nature minimising any privacy concerns. The benefits outweigh any concerns in proportionality calculations.

The Home Office (2018a) estimate that about 80,000 BWV cameras are in operational use within police forces in England and Wales. Officers will usually activate the recording when:

- *stopping vehicles;*
- *arresting suspects;*
- *conducting stop searches;*
- *using force;*
- *conducting searches;*
- *attending domestic abuse incidents.*

The data can benefit investigations through recording:

- *first accounts from victims, suspects or witnesses;*
- *identification;*
- *conversations with members of the public;*
- *decisions and actions of the officer;*
- *physical and mental state of people;*
- *demeanour of people;*
- *actions of people;*
- *prevailing atmosphere;*
- *location of evidence;*
- *criminal activity.*

(Home Office, 2018a)

It is important to realise that BWV complements traditional evidence-collection techniques; it does not replace them. The doubts of a minority of officers about BWV are countered by the increased support for decision making provided by the recordings.

BWV has featured in a number of evidence-based policing pieces of research (Chapter 9 refers to evidence-based policing) (Owens et al, 2014; Ward, 2020). The analysis of BWV in operational settings identified benefits in gathering evidence, providing context and capturing comments in an efficient dynamic manner appropriate to a wide variety of situations. The ability to provide evidence of professional actions and demeanour contributes to public confidence in policing. In the combative environment of an adversarial justice system, footage of incidents and police interactions must surely be the best evidence available.

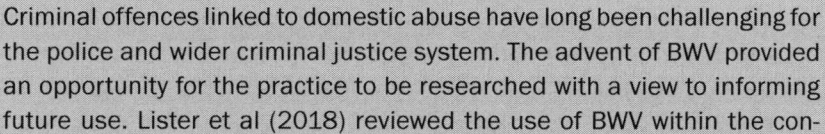

EVIDENCE-BASED POLICING

Criminal offences linked to domestic abuse have long been challenging for the police and wider criminal justice system. The advent of BWV provided an opportunity for the practice to be researched with a view to informing future use. Lister et al (2018) reviewed the use of BWV within the context of domestic abuse in both urban and predominantly rural force areas. The ability to gather evidence from the scene, including contextual settings, record the impact of events, produce material capable of being reviewed by various actors in the criminal justice system, and address the vulnerabilities of victims and witnesses in providing evidence were all recognised as valuable factors that BWV brings to investigations. Ancillary benefits, such as the contribution officers felt BWV made to calming situations down and supporting both corroboration and challenges of accounts, only adds to the device's value. The advent of BWV has brought great benefits to policing and will continue to do so.

PROFILING

Criminal profiling gained publicity through fictional depictions such as *Cracker* (1993–1995), *The Silence of the Lambs* (1991) and *Criminal Minds* (2005–2020). Criminal profiling is defined as the practice of predicting personality, behavioural and demographic characteristics based on crime scene evidence (Hicks and Sales, 2006, p 67). Williamson (2007) notes the benefits of considering profilers or behavioural investigative advisors (BIAs) in the following areas:

- crime scenes;

- predictive profiling;

- prioritising suspects;

- investigative suggestions;

- interviewing strategies;

- media strategies;

- familial DNA strategies.

Canter (2010) describes an investigative stage where suspects remain unidentified and inferences are made on the basis of information collected (see Chapter 3). These inferences may reveal hitherto unexplored avenues of investigation or provide greater focus on existing avenues of enquiry. This stage is often referred to as 'profiling' and is a relatively recent addition to the investigator's armoury, established in the 1980s and 1990s. It is difficult to draw inferences from individual events; linked or serial offending is much more likely to reveal behavioural factors which will inform inferences. It is important to realise that profiling is guidance rather than proof. The suggestions are subject to many variables and are exactly that – suggestions.

Profiling seeks identifiable patterns, which are likely to evolve in crime series or through repeat offending. Criminals learn from experience as we all do; a burglar who has been previously caught through fingerprints is unlikely to make the same mistake again. This presents the advice that what is missing from a scene is as important as what is present. Elements of forensic awareness portray professional knowledge that often comes from an offending history. This is a valuable point in identifying a suspect.

Profiling successes are represented by the 1987 conviction of John Duffy. Duffy, an active rapist and murderer for at least five years, was convicted of seven offences and suspected of many more. It is acknowledged that profiling was a major contributor to his apprehension. The crimes involved attacks at night in North London on or near railway trains; young girls were accosted while waiting for or leaving trains near stations. He would then commit rape and murder his victims. A profiler joined the enquiry team, analysing all material to create a suggested profile of the offender and allowing enquiry teams to focus lists of potential suspects to more manageable numbers. Contrast this with the investigation into the murder of Rachel Nickell in 1992, where police were guided by a profiler in an undercover operation to catch an identified suspect. The over-reliance on profiling at the expense of other investigative techniques led to officers concentrating on Colin Stagg, a prosecution which was dismissed by the court before the successful subsequent identification of Robert Napper as the murderer.

Canter (2010, p 117) outlines five questions arising from a crime to which profiling may contribute answers.

1. What does the crime indicate about the intelligence and knowledge of the offender?

2. What does it suggest about the degree of planning or impulsivity?

3. How does the offender interact with victims?

4. What do the actions indicate about the degree of familiarity with the situation or circumstances of the crime?

5. What particular skills does the offender have?

MULTI-AGENCY INVESTIGATIONS

The benefits of a multi-agency approach can be evidenced through the creation of the Multi-agency Public Protection Arrangements (MAPPA) in the Criminal Justice and Court Services Act 2000. Harnessing the abilities of complementary agencies towards a common target multiplies the effectiveness of any investigation. During investigations you will find yourself working with a range of statutory and non-governmental agencies in the investigative environment. The Prison Service, Health and Safety Executive, Environment Agency, Her Majesty's Revenue and Customs, Border Agency and Fire and Rescue Services are just some of the common partners. On-going developments in the digital environment will increase the challenges of working with multiple investigative partners across a range of jurisdictions. A pragmatic approach of involving the most appropriate support for specific challenges flows through the methods of support exemplified in this chapter. Each partnership will bring data sharing and working practice challenges. Agreed objectives and memorandums of understanding (MOU) detailing responsibilities are vital. Fleming and Rhodes (2005) discuss how tensions over objectives and roles may introduce antagonism in multi-agency working. Recognising agency-specific requirements in investigative operations is important; as a criminal investigator, your evidential requirements may differ from an agency whose primary role is to safeguard victims. Lack of attention to these differing requirements may lead to tension and will not provide the fullest picture available. Policing investigations encompass far more than the mainstream view of crime. The following policing spotlight draws your attention to a multi-agency response that was required for a wide-ranging powerful situation that impacted a significant number of people nationwide.

POLICING SPOTLIGHT

The foot and mouth disease epidemic of 2001 brought a requirement for intelligence, investigation and enforcement together on a national basis. Animal movement and destruction orders were introduced. Public rights of way were closed. Exclusion zones made travel difficult in some areas. The then Ministry of Agriculture, Fisheries and Food (now called the Department of Environment, Food and Rural Affairs), army, veterinary services, transport companies, retail sector, National Farmers' Union and many others were joined by the police in enforcing regulations, gathering intelligence and investigating breaches. The epidemic lasted for nine months, and over 6 million animals were culled to stop the spread. As with many crisis situations, initial actions were dynamic in nature. Lessons learnt included the requirement for emergency planning, which is now enshrined in legislation through the Civil Contingencies Act 2004. The knowledge and skills of police officers often see them taking an important role in multi-agency operations.

EXPERTS

Engaging with this book confirms the wide range of situations investigators will encounter. Accessing the best information to gain the best understanding is the mark of a professional investigator; this is where the use of experts comes in. It would be impossible to list the infinite number of scenarios experts can contribute to. Some examples are used to show how they contribute and what issues you must address to maximise the benefit of expert advisors.

POLICING SPOTLIGHT

In 1997, leisure divers in Coniston Water, Cumbria, discovered a body; enquiries revealed this to be the remains of Carol Park, who had been reported missing 21 years previously. This investigation, which resulted in the conviction of Carol's husband Gordon Park, became known as the 'Lady in the Lake' case. Alongside the challenges of investigating historical events, the case may be noted for the challenges to expert opinion provided to the court. Experts in currents, sailing, knots and geology contributed to the investigation and trial. Their views have been challenged in the trial court and through subsequent appeals as well as in media and through general commentary. Researching the coverage of the investigation will provide you with an inkling of the challenges expert opinion provides.

Information is central to all investigations, and this book details a variety of methods designed to maximise the success of information gathering. From the golden hour to defence statements, all will provide material to influence or direct your enquiries. Interpreting the material gathered cannot rely solely on police officers, and subject experts are key to effectively analysing information. The murder of Carol Park, described in the previous policing spotlight, exemplifies the range of experts who may assist an enquiry. The Crown Prosecution Service (CPS) (2019b) provides a non-exhaustive list of commonly encountered areas of expertise:

- DNA;
- ear prints;
- facial mapping, video evidence;
- fingerprints;
- footwear impressions;
- forensic anthropology;
- forensic archaeology;
- forensic pathology;
- handwriting;
- hypnosis;
- medical;
- non-accidental head injury;
- autopsies;
- voice recognition;
- gait analysis.

The breadth of possible experts who can contribute is as wide as your imagination, and the Carol Park murder and drugs operation discussed in Critical thinking activity 6.2 illustrate the diversity of skills that you could call upon. The National Crime Agency (NCA) maintains a database of available experts; the nature of expert contributors is such that no database can include all possible disciplines.

Credibility is important in all witnesses. Before engaging an expert, you should ensure they are qualified to pass opinion in their field. Accurate briefings are imperative, as no expert can pass opinion without access to the full picture. You may need to emphasise the confidentiality of your investigation, and it is important to remember that expertise in a particular field does not equate to expertise in the conduct of an investigation. Many professional disciplines have their own professional jargon (policing is the ideal example), and the role of an expert is to provide an insight into areas in which your investigative colleagues or a court have little experience. Discussions with your expert will identify where this occurs. Any explanations will need to be understood by colleagues, the judiciary and ordinary people in the guise of a jury, so it is important to make sure that any material provided by the expert meets this test.

Experts may also feature in dual aspects of an investigation. For example, in the earlier description of Winthroping, the advice guided lines of enquiry and the expertise itself informed the court of the basis of the enquiries. The Carol Park murder experts both advised the investigative team and provided evidence of opinion to the court.

BEST EVIDENCE

The introduction to Chapter 5 outlined the concept of best evidence as defined in *Omychund v Barker* 1744 in which Lord Harwicke stated that '*no evidence was admissible unless it was the best that nature would allow*'. The general rule in law is that witnesses should only testify to matters in their personal knowledge, concentrating on fact and excluding opinion.

In the interests of providing 'best evidence' to the court, certain exemptions to this evidence of fact rule may be made to allow a court to hear evidence of opinion. Part 19 of the Criminal Procedure Rules confirms that in order for an expert to provide their opinion to a court, that opinion should be objective, unbiased and within the expert's area of knowledge. Opinion must be based on their knowledge, experience and expertise, and the fact the expert is working for the prosecution or the defence should be immaterial in their findings. In court hearings, the opinion should be of assistance. Neither a court nor an investigator should be bound by the expert's opinion, and it is important that their opinion is considered alongside all other material of evidence. The experiences involving Sir Roy Meadows, as detailed in the next policing spotlight feature, show what can occur when there is an over-reliance on expert opinion.

CRITICAL THINKING ACTIVITY 6.2

LEVEL 6

As a 'drug squad' detective in 1990s, I (Iain Stainton) was called to give expert evidence to court on the values, amounts, packaging, prices and availability of controlled drugs. My expertise came from experience and involvement rather than formal qualifications. This expert evidence was often challenged by other 'experts' but was acceptable to the court.

Drawing on the case of *R v Hodges* [2003], imagine you are found in such a situation, and critically analyse your approach to issues of witness credibility and allegations of bias.

POLICING SPOTLIGHT

Expert advisors are crucial to investigations; in complex rapidly developing situations, no investigative team can include those with the requisite knowledge to address all likelihoods. The influence on lines of enquiry can be many and varied. The opinions passed can assist a court to understand situations outside their experience. On a number of occasions, experts have subsequently been found to lack credibility, or to be simply wrong. We will now explore some examples of this.

Trevor Bates contributed to a number of enquiries and was listed on the NCA database as a computer expert, particularly with respect to people suspected of accessing abuse material online. He complemented this with contributions to police training programmes. It transpired that the degree he claimed to hold and military service he referred to were false. Jessica Rees was a lip-reading expert who quoted degree qualifications she had never completed. One of the most infamous circumstances surrounds the expert evidence of Sir Roy Meadows, a respected paediatrician who provided expert opinion in several murder cases involving the deaths of young children. It transpired that the statistical calculations his theories were based upon were wrong. This led to several successful appeals for miscarriages of justice as a result of his opinion evidence to the courts.

The concept of experts leads us to engage with their advice, and evidence from experienced, highly qualified individuals is persuasive. As an investigator, how will you satisfy yourself that the experts you consult will contribute positively to your investigation?

CONCLUSION

Locating, analysing and drawing conclusions from material is key to an investigation. Where material is outside the knowledge and experience of the investigator, it would be remiss not to seek the strongest advice available. The accompanying code of practice to the Criminal Procedure and Investigations Act 1996 states '*In conducting an investigation, the investigator should pursue all reasonable lines of inquiry, whether these point towards or away from the suspect*'. This confirms the importance of not disregarding reasonable lines of enquiry.

SUMMARY OF KEY CONCEPTS

The contribution of police and non-police experts broadens the scope of your investigations to encompass the best available advice and analysis to the widest range of situations. Expert witnesses provide informed opinion to assist a court in decision making. Expert input should be:

- credible;
- objective;
- pragmatic;
- based on demonstrable knowledge and experience.

As with all material, your role is to evaluate the source and the material itself to assess its reliability. We stress the importance of the witness element of the expert witness in this calculation. You are drawing on others' expertise to complement your expertise in investigation so ensure you are not unduly influenced by the status of an expert.

CHECK YOUR KNOWLEDGE

1. Body-worn video recording equipment should be turned on when…?

2. How would you apply the concept of 'best evidence' to your investigations?

3. What attributes are vital in experts who contribute to criminal investigations?

4. You have lawfully seized a mobile phone during an investigation and want to extract data from it. What advice do the principles of digital investigation suggest you follow?

Sample answers to these questions are provided at the end of the book.

FURTHER READING

R (Bridges) v Chief Constable of South Wales Police and Ors [2020]. EWCA 1058. [online] Available at: www.judiciary.uk/wp-content/uploads/2020/08/R-Bridges-v-CC-South-Wales-ors-Judgment.pdf (accessed 12 November 2021).
The case of Bridges provides contemporary commentary of the legal approach to facial biometrics.

The College of Policing's 'What Works Network' provides a searchable database of policing research: https://whatworks.college.police.uk/Pages/default.aspx

CHAPTER 7
COVERT METHODS

LEARNING OBJECTIVES

AFTER READING THIS CHAPTER YOU WILL BE ABLE TO:

- differentiate between types of surveillance;
- categorise human information sources;
- summarise proportionality characteristics in investigative techniques;
- justify necessity criteria in covert deployments.

INTRODUCTION

The nature of covert methods requires levels of deceit and fraudulent behaviour which would be anathema to the public's expectations of police behaviours. Social and ethical debates such as those which delayed the introduction of detectives during the establishment of the Metropolitan Police in 1829 still persist in contemporary society. Covert policing methods emphasise public fears of the state spying on people by virtue of their clandestine, intrusive nature. The recognition of the effect intrusive covert methods have on the public's view of policing led to the introduction of levels of accountability rarely encountered in more mainstream investigative activity. The necessity of covert deployments is established through many years of practice. Necessity criteria are such an inherent part of covert arrangements that they feature throughout this section. Policing models centre on the social contract, a hypothetical agreement between citizens and state where certain freedoms are surrendered in exchange for the protection of the state. Rousseau and Cranston (2005) and Neyroud and Beckley (2001) refer to consent and balance within the social contract, factors which will be explored alongside permissive legislation, surveillance, covert human intelligence sources (CHISs) and the influence of the Human Rights Act 1998.

OVERVIEW OF COVERT METHODS

Covert methods such as surveillance refer to investigative techniques where the subjects are unaware it is taking place. Legislation differentiates between surveillance and informant-led techniques; these will be explored individually in this chapter. Important aspects such as proportionality, necessity and ethics are common to all covert methods and will be discussed accordingly.

Traditional surveillance techniques are relatively low tech; the evolution of surveillance devices and widespread monitoring methods such as automatic number plate recognition (ANPR) and facial recognition systems contribute much to the contemporary surveillance realm. However, this chapter concentrates on the knowledge and understanding needed to deploy surveillance and covert human intelligence sources (CHISs) in an operational environment.

Chapter 1 refers to the legitimacy of investigative actions, confirming the significance of effective, morally justifiable techniques to police–public relationships. In common with other policing powers, such as stop and search, the unwritten social contract that supports policing by consent is dependent upon a professional approach to maintain trust between the police and the public. Traditionally governed by policy and guidelines, the move to permissive legislation such as the Regulation of Investigatory Powers Act 2000 (RIPA) and the Human Rights Act 1998 now provides the foundation for covert practices.

The role of policing in protecting rights must not be contradicted by unwarranted interference in those same rights. Waldron (2003, p 192) states that:

> *The apparent need to balance or offset competing values and interests when contemplating otherwise morally harmful conduct is an area that deserves robust scrutiny and requires critical thinking and faultless logic.*

The nature of covert methods results in elements of coercion, deception and manipulation occurring. This contradicts the long-held principle of policing by consent (Reith, 1956). In his 2004 report to the parliamentary committee, the surveillance commissioner Richard Thomas claimed:

> *Surveillance is an inescapable part of life in the UK. Every time we make a telephone call, send an email, browse the internet or even walk down our local high street, our actions may be monitored and recorded. To respond to crime, combat the threat of terrorism and improve administrative efficiency, successive UK governments have gradually constructed one of the most extensive and technologically advanced systems in the world. At the same time similar developments in the private sector have contributed to a profound change in the character of life.*

This report gave rise to the term 'surveillance society' used to describe the overall situation. Societal views are emphasised in the critical thinking activity later in this chapter, which encourages you to consider perceptions of privacy in a mass surveillance society.

The use of surveillance and informants as investigative techniques are well established. It can be argued that the existence of informants can be traced to biblical times, while Bentham's panoptical approach to crime management originated in the eighteenth century. Although covert methods are used in both reactive and proactive environments, the widespread adoption of intelligence-led policing throughout the 1990s accentuated the use of covert strategies in pre-emptive operations.

The common law principle that 'anything which is not forbidden is allowed' reinforced the historic practice of governing covert methods through non-legislative policy and guidance. This was a situation which predominated prior to the Regulation of Investigatory Powers Act 2000 (RIPA) and illustrated by the influential case of *Malone v UK* [1984]. RIPA and the Human Rights Act 1998 are now the dominant pieces of legislation in the covert environment. The next sections provide an appreciation of these laws.

It is important to note that the covert methods this chapter concentrates on may be appropriate in any investigation; they are not unique to serious matters. As such, all officers will benefit from the working knowledge this chapter provides.

The requirement for covert methods occurs when more traditional investigative techniques are unable to provide the levels of access covert methods provide; by their very nature these tactics will intrude on human rights, which is a challenge that will be examined in the next section.

HUMAN RIGHTS ACT 1998

Human rights are not a recent introduction to policing. The UK was a signatory to the European Convention on Human Rights in 1951, although the rights themselves were not incorporated into English law until the creation of the Human Rights Act (HRA) 1998. The 1998 act allows people to seek redress for breaches of their rights in a British court as opposed to relying on European courts, as was the case previously. Legislation must now be compatible with the 1998 act and public bodies are required to respect the rights contained therein. The HRA contains a series of articles, each addressing a particular right.

Human rights are classed as absolute, limited or qualified, and can be defined as follows.

- Absolute rights (A) must not be breached in any circumstances. Articles 3, 4 and 7 are absolute rights.

- Limited rights (L) may be interfered with in specified circumstances. For example, Article 5 may be breached if a person is convicted of an offence where imprisonment is an option for punishment. Section 1 of the Police and Criminal Evidence Act 1984 allows a person to be detained for the purpose of a stop and search.

- Qualified rights (Q) such as Articles 8, 9, 10, 11 and 14 may be interfered with where the aim of the interference is to protect the rights of others.

The list below shows how each of the HRA articles are classified.

- Article 2: Right to life (L).

- Article 3: Freedom from torture, inhuman or degrading treatment (A).

- Article 4: Freedom from slavery and forced labour (A).

- Article 5: Right to liberty and security (L).

- Article 6: Right to a fair trial (L).

- Article 7: No punishment without law (A).

- Article 8: Respect for private and family life and correspondence (Q).

- Article 9: Freedom of thought, belief and religion (Q).

- Article 10: Freedom of expression (Q).

- Article 11: Freedom of assembly and association (Q).

- Article 12: Right to marry and start a family (L).

- Article 14: Protection from discrimination in respect of these rights and freedoms (Q).

Such breaches are dependent on balancing the interests of the wider community against an individual's rights. This balancing theme will be returned to later in the chapter in the section about 'necessity'. The interference must have a basis in law and be proportionate and necessary. This requirement for a 'basis in law' led to the creation of the Regulation of Investigatory Powers Act 2000 (RIPA). Policy and guidance previously relied upon when considering covert techniques such as surveillance and informant use did not provide the basis in law required to legally breach human rights such as Article 8. RIPA introduced legislation permitting surveillance, covert human intelligence sources (CHISs) and accessing communications data. This chapter will concentrate on the surveillance and CHIS elements of the act.

The implications for policing are significant. As a public body, officers must respect the articles and protect the rights on citizens' behalf. Articles 5 and 6 align with investigative practice, ensuring your actions will not jeopardise a fair trial. Articles 9, 10 and 11 may feature when policing protest. These are referred to as positive or negative obligations. For example, the state has a negative duty not to breach Article 2 and a positive duty to protect citizens identified as at risk. The case of Ahmet Osman detailed in the next policing spotlight feature provides an example of this.

POLICING SPOTLIGHT

The influence of the Human Rights Act 1998 on policing can be illustrated by the case heard by the ECtHR – *Osman v United Kingdom* (Application 23452/94) (1998). This case gave rise to the use of 'Osman warnings', which have been issued over 2000 times since 2012. The case is based on a failure to protect Article 2 of the HRA, the right to life.

The situation began in 1987 when a teacher, Mr Paget-Lewis, developed an attachment to a 14 year-old boy at school, Ahmet Osman. The police visited the school several times, but no action was recorded. Following Paget-Lewis's suspension from the school, the Osman family suffered from a series of attacks on their property. Paget-Lewis was interviewed and no further action ensued. His suspension had ceased at this point and he returned to school. Following a further incident, Paget-Lewis revealed he felt self-destructive and was 'thinking of doing a Hungerford' (a mass killing which took place in the town in 1987). The police were made aware. A decision was made to arrest him on 17 December; officers visiting his home discovered he was at work. The education authority was asked to inform him to contact the police. Paget-Lewis did not return to work and spent time travelling in the UK. It was later discovered he stole a firearm during this period. On 7 March, Paget-Lewis shot and killed Ahmet's father and wounded Ahmet before travelling to his former headmaster's home, where he shot and killed the headmaster's son and wounded the headmaster. He was arrested and subsequently convicted of the deaths. This case was based on the alleged negligence of the authorities in failing to protect the Osmans, as outlined in Article 2 of the HRA. The European court found that there had been no breach of Article 2 of the HRA, which obliged authorities to take positive action to protect where a threat was known. Paget-Lewis's actions could not have been predicted. The court found no breach, but the situation led to the introduction of Osman warnings where the police make individuals aware that intelligence suggests a threat to their safety, but no grounds for arrest exist. This confirms the duality of policing in respecting and protecting articles of the HRA.

Any discussion on covert methodology will bring Article 8 to the fore. You may ask how any investigation can take place without breaching rights, and this is where an understanding of the legislation will be of benefit.

REGULATION OF INVESTIGATORY POWERS ACT 2000

RIPA is referred to as permissive legislation where actions which breach law (HRA) are permitted in tightly controlled situations. As the previous section outlines, RIPA acknowledges surveillance and CHIS activity is likely to breach Article 8 of the HRA. RIPA created an accountable system of authorisation for such practices. Concepts of necessity and proportionality are important elements to any authorisation, which will now be considered along with collateral intrusion.

NECESSITY

The notion of necessity is central to activities authorised under RIPA. The 2000 Act outlines statutory grounds which amount to necessity criteria as:

a) *in the interests of national security;*

b) *for the purpose of preventing or detecting crime or preventing disorder;*

c) *in the interests of the economic well-being of the United Kingdom;*

d) *in the interests of public safety;*

e) *for the purpose of protecting public health;*

f) *for the purpose of assessing or collecting any tax, duty, levy or other imposition, contribution or charge payable to a government department; or*

g) *for any purpose (not falling within (a) to (f)) which is specified by an order made by the Secretary of State.*

(RIPA 2000, s 28(3))

In simple terms, is your proposed action necessary to achieve the identified aims? Any reasoning supporting the claim of necessity must be objective and precise, acknowledging that no less intrusive manner of achieving the aim exists. The criminal investigation construct meets a social need, and you need to demonstrate how your proposed activity contributes to this. The importance of the necessity element is illustrated by Neyroud and Beckley's (2001) claim that necessity criteria link to democracy itself. The longstanding and evocative case of Dudley and Stephens emphasises the prominence of necessity in law. It also illustrates that necessity can be associated with a variety of investigative tactics. The critical thinking activity that follows asks you to link activities to RIPA necessity criteria.

POLICING SPOTLIGHT

The legal view of necessity has been demonstrated for over 100 years by the historic case of *R v Dudley and Stephens* [1884].

In July 1883, the yacht Mignonette was sunk off the coast of South Africa. Four members of the crew, Thomas Dudley, Edwin Stephens, Edmund Brooks and Richard Parker, launched a lifeboat and survived the sinking. With little food or water, Dudley and Stephens discussed killing Parker, the youngest member and only one without family who was judged to be ill and near death. Brooks claimed never to have agreed to such a course of action. Stephens subsequently held Parker while Dudley killed him. The three cannibalised Parker. The group were rescued by a passing ship on 6 September. The remains in the lifeboat and their accounts confirmed what had happened. Dudley and Stephens were charged with murder based on their confessions. Brooks was not charged, the lack of a confession meaning the only evidence was that of the co-defendants which was inadmissible at the time.

The defence was based on the perceived necessity of their actions, drawing on theories of utilitarianism that the group would benefit from the obviously immoral action in order to survive. Dudley and Stephens were found guilty, giving rise to the following quote.

> *We are often compelled to set up standards we cannot reach ourselves, and to lay down rules which we could not ourselves satisfy. But a man has no right to declare temptation to be an excuse, though he might himself have yielded to it, nor allow compassion for the criminal to change or weaken in any manner the legal definition of the crime.*
>
> (Lord Coleridge in Dudley and Stephens (1884) 14 Q.B.D. 273)

This situation was mirrored many years later in what Klockars (1985) referred to as 'Dirty Harry' policing, where 'dirty' means were used to achieve a desired outcome. This is a situation referred to as 'noble cause corruption' in the Stephen Lawrence Independent Review (Ellison, 2014).

CRITICAL THINKING ACTIVITY 7.1

LEVEL 4

Can you identify specific policing situations where the RIPA necessity criteria (a) to (e) outlined earlier would be appropriate?

Your proposed course of action must be necessary, representing an objective decision, and alternatives should be considered and discarded as unviable. The necessity element is specific to your proposition; the RIPA necessity criteria are an important foundation, but you should be prepared to explain how the identified technique will contribute to you achieving the desired aim. This allows you to move to the proportionality of your application.

PROPORTIONALITY

When a surveillance or CHIS deployment has been deemed necessary, you should then address the proportionality question. Authority cannot be approved if the necessity case is not made. Proportionality is a balancing equation contrasting the seriousness of the intrusion against the investigative need. For example, while it is feasible to deploy intrusive surveillance in support of an investigation into criminal damage through graffitiing, it would not be proportionate; no necessity could be proven and it is unlikely to contribute any relevant information that could not be obtained through less intrusive means.

The CHIS and Surveillance Codes of Practice (Home Office, 2018b) introduce five elements to assist in deciding if an action is proportional.

1. Balance the size and scope of the proposed activity against the gravity and extent of the perceived crime or harm.

2. Explain how and why the methods to be adopted will cause the least possible intrusion on the subject and others.

3. Will the conduct to be authorised have any implications for the privacy of others; if so why is it proportionate to proceed?

4. Evidence as far as reasonably practicable what other methods have been considered and why were they not implemented or were unsuccessful.

5. Consider if the activity represents an appropriate use of the legislation and is a reasonable way of obtaining the information sought.

Starmer (1999) advanced five elements of proportionality which tend to confirm those contained in the codes of practice.

1. Whether relevant or sufficient reasons have been advanced.

2. Whether less restrictive alternatives are available.

3. Whether there was a procedural fairness in the decision making.

4. Whether safeguards against abuse exist.

5. Whether the restriction destroys the very essence of a right.

He describes proportionality as *'the fair balance between protecting individual rights and the interests of the community at large'* (Starmer, 1999, p 270). Intrusive activities will often be practically achievable, but will they be proportionate to the circumstances? Sections 28 and 29 of RIPA confirm the importance of proportionality, confirming that proposed surveillance or CHIS activity shall not be authorised unless deemed proportionate.

An often-quoted maxim is that of the 'maximum' speed limit; that limit may not be appropriate for conditions prevailing at the time. Consider this alongside your covert methods knowledge. The technique may be legal, but is it proportionate? You should adopt the least intrusive level possible to achieve your aims. Take a contextual rather than a literal approach to your planning.

EVIDENCE-BASED POLICING

You may have noticed the term 'reasonable' appears throughout legislation. From the Police and Criminal Evidence Act 1984 (PACE), section 1, stop and search, section 24, powers of arrest, and section 117, use of force, all refer to reasonable grounds. The dishonesty test emanating from *Ivey v Genting Casinos* [2017] refers to the views of a reasonable person. Originally referred to as the 'man on the Clapham omnibus', this fictional representation of an ordinary person frequently features in law, representing an objective test where the conduct in question is compared to how a reasonable person would behave in similar circumstances. This may be contextual, dependent upon the circumstances or the expected expertise of the person whose conduct is being considered. Working on the basis that you are a reasonable person, if a course of action seems excessive to you, it is unlikely to meet a test of reasonableness and you are advised to revisit your proposal. As an investigator, Iain Stainton recommends the reasonableness test when planning any covert deployments. If the proposal seems unreasonable, it is unlikely to be proportionate to the circumstances you are investigating.

RIPA sets out the legal requirements that need to be in place for a covert activity to be lawful. To ensure that you add proportionality, accountability and necessity to your deliberations, applying the mnemonic PLAN may be of assistance. When you assess the suitability of a covert technique, you should ask yourself if your proposal is:

- **P**roportionate;

- **L**egal;

- **A**ccountable;

- **N**ecessary.

If one of the elements is missing, then a re-evaluation may be called for.

COLLATERAL INTRUSION

The 2018 surveillance codes of practice raise the likelihood of third parties featuring in proposed activities as an important factor in authorising surveillance activity. This is known as collateral intrusion. Authorised activity will be focused on the subject, although unconnected third parties are likely to feature. It would be almost impossible to conduct surveillance without some collateral intrusion whereby private information of unconnected parties would result. Discussions with relatives or neighbours, retail transactions and normal daily business see us interact with a wide variety of people. You must develop an assessment for dealing with this, which should address the proportionality of this risk occurring, acknowledging its existence and outlining your proposed actions.

SURVEILLANCE

RIPA defines two forms of surveillance: directed and intrusive. Section 26(2) of RIPA defines directed surveillance as:

Covert but not intrusive and is undertaken:

a) For the purposes of a specific investigation or a specific operation

b) In such a manner as is likely to result in the obtaining of private information about a person (whether or not one specifically identified for the purposes of the investigation or operation); and

138 CRIMINAL INVESTIGATION

c) *Otherwise than by way of an immediate response to events or circumstances the nature of which is such that it would not be reasonably practicable for an authorisation under this Part to be sought for the carrying out of the surveillance.*

Intrusive surveillance is covert surveillance that:

a) *is carried out in relation to anything taking place on any residential premises or in a private vehicle, and*

b) *involves the presence of an individual on the premises or in the vehicle or is carried out by means of a surveillance device.*

General duties may very well see you responding to situations involving discreet observations. Situations like this may well be regarded as immediate responses, which while having elements of covertness do not amount to directed or intrusive surveillance. Using CCTV as part of your reactive investigation will not be considered as surveillance. If you are considering using a CCTV system to monitor activities, you are advised to seek advice as this may amount to surveillance. Figure 7.1 provides a reference point when assessing which, if any, surveillance authority is required.

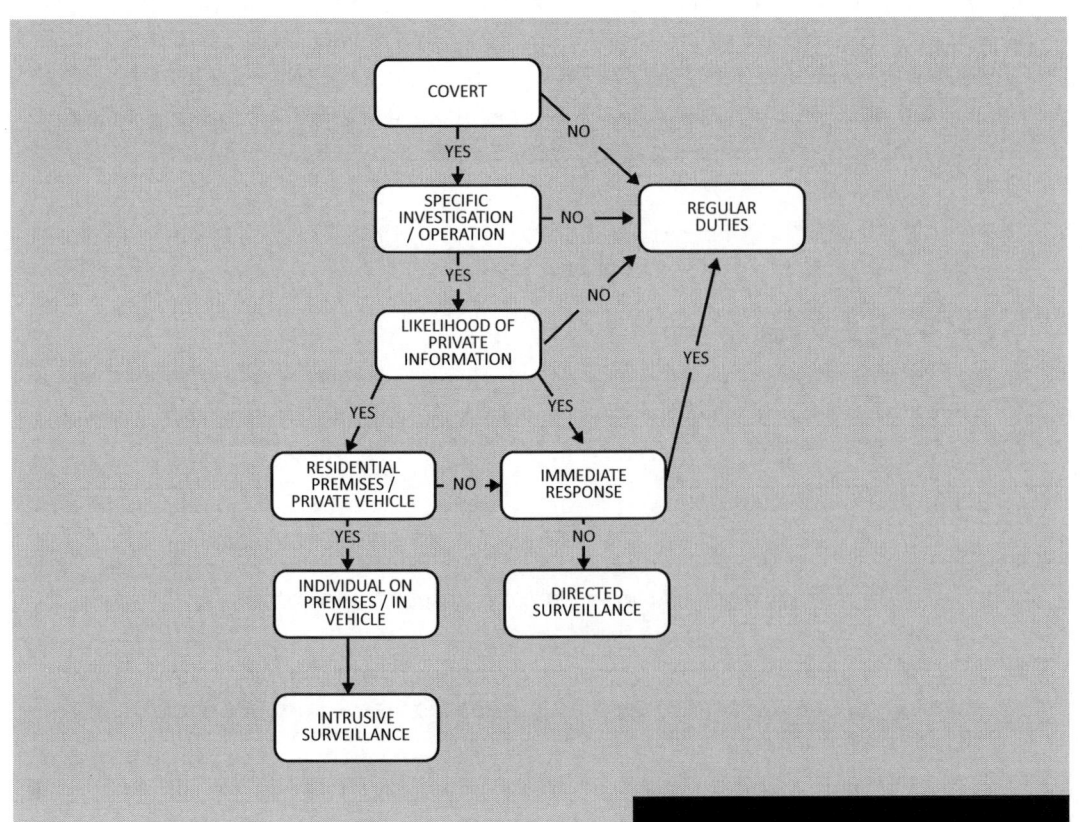

Figure 7.1 Surveillance flow chart

The likelihood of obtaining private information is central to surveillance. RIPA provides a broad definition of private information: '*any information relating to a person's private or family life*' (RIPA 2000, s 26(2)). The calculation of whether you will obtain private information should include all information you may obtain, including through collateral intrusion. A series of individual pieces of information may amount to private information when assessed as a whole.

The nature of intrusive surveillance introduces an elevated level of intrusion, referring to surveillance in locations where an increased sense of privacy is assumed. Intrusive surveillance is often accompanied by a requirement to enter or interfere with property. This is known as property interference; the power to do this is contained in the Police Act 1997. Any authorisation must be allied to the relevant RIPA authority for intrusive surveillance. The authorising officer (AO) must be satisfied with the necessity and proportionality of the proposed interference before granting authority, which must be further scrutinised by a judicial commissioner or surveillance commissioner, providing a dual element to the accountability in recognition of the increased levels of intrusion. These discussions focus on situations you will encounter in the early stages of your investigative career. Details on other, more intrusive, techniques can be found in the recommended reading at the end of the chapter should you wish to develop your knowledge of this specialised field.

CRITICAL THINKING ACTIVITY 7.2

LEVEL 6

In the age of mass surveillance, evaluate whether two people holding a conversation in a public area have any expectation of privacy. Would the content of the conversation represent 'private information' as defined by RIPA?

COVERT HUMAN INTELLIGENCE SOURCES

Covert human intelligence sources (CHISs) have been referred to by many terms, both professional and derogatory (grass, tout, rat, nark, snitch being some of the repeatable ones).

It is important that appropriate terminology is used in all investigative matters. It is easy to be drawn into an environment where jargon predominates; however, this manner of speech does not indicate your depth of knowledge, quite the opposite. Something as simple as a derogatory phrase may create a harmful impression, which is not always easy to undo. This book will refer only to CHISs. A CHIS has the potential to bring value to investigations and intelligence gathering in a way few other techniques can match. The human element also brings a variety of challenges.

Section 26(8) of RIPA defines a CHIS as a person who:

- *establishes or maintains a personal or other relationship with a person for the covert purpose of facilitating the doing of anything falling within paragraph (b) or (c);*

- *covertly uses such a relationship to obtain information or provide access to any information to another person; or*

- *covertly discloses information obtained by the use of such a relationship, or as a consequence of the existence of such a relationship.*

The relationship aspect of the definition mirrors the private information aspect of surveillance in its importance to assessing the situation and the requirement for authorisation to be sought.

Establishing a relationship should be given its ordinary meaning of creating or initiating. Maintaining introduces a period to the relationship; no repetition is required although no timescales are mentioned, confirming the relationship once established may be short or long depending on the covert deployment aims and objectives. The manipulation referred to at the beginning of this chapter will be found in the covert operation of the relationship in order to gain information.

Authorisation for a CHIS refers to use and conduct; normally both are present in applications. Use refers to any action to 'induce, ask or assist' a person to act as a CHIS. Conduct comprises the steps taken in pursuance of their role as a CHIS.

The growth of digital investigations raises questions about whether online activities amount to surveillance of CHIS deployments. If the action is conducted covertly for a specific operation or investigation and is likely to result in private information being gathered, you should consider directed surveillance authorities. If someone is acting covertly in establishing or maintaining relationships to obtain and disclose information, you should consider their status to answer the question of whether they are a helpful member of public, witness or CHIS.

COVERTNESS

Surveillance and CHIS definitions both refer to covertness; the 2000 act defines this as *'actions... carried out in a manner calculated to ensure that persons subject to surveillance are unaware that it is taking place'* (RIPA 2000, s 26(9)). Covertness in respect of CHIS applies to the relationship aspect, confirming that if a relationship is maintained or established or disclosures carried out in a manner calculated to ensure one party is unaware of the purpose, this also amounts to covert behaviour.

AUTHORITY LEVELS

To gain authority to deploy these covert methods, application to an authorising officer (AO) is required. Table 7.1 details the position of policing AOs relative to the nature of the application. You will notice that as the level of intrusion increases so too does the seniority of the AO. They must be satisfied that the proposed conduct is both necessary and proportionate, along with in-depth justification and risk assessment of the methods to be used. Such levels of intrusion require oversight to maintain confidence in the police to use such powers.

Table 7.1 Authorising officer levels of seniority

Authorising officer level – police	
Directed surveillance	Superintendent
Intrusive surveillance	Chief officer and judicial commissioner
Property interference	Chief officer
Covert human intelligence source	Superintendent

REFLECTIVE PRACTICE 7.1

LEVEL 5

Having spent a considerable part of my policing career in covert environments, I (Iain Stainton) believe the CHIS represents one of the most intrusive techniques.

A valuable exercise is to evaluate the risks of deployment to your organisation, the investigation and the individuals in question. Reflect on the potential risks of deploying a drug user into a 'county lines' environment. Do you feel this hypothetical situation is proportionate?

CONCLUSION

This chapter has concentrated on covert methods from a policing aspect. It should be noted that RIPA applies to all public authorities. The full list of relevant public authorities can be found in schedule 1, part 1 of the 2000 act.

The use of police powers deployed to the disadvantage of others always requires moral consideration, even in instances where that police power is prescribed. The perception of fairness of covert activity is difficult to achieve in a public environment. Although long established, surveillance and CHIS tactics are associated with protecting rights through morally distasteful methods and a maverick style of policing.

Reference the contemporary legislative environment and you will see this is far from the case. A tightly controlled accountability regime accompanies covert deployments. Surveillance and CHIS represent effective responses to particular investigative challenges. You are using intrusive techniques; it would be paradoxical if an authorising regime were not intrusive into an applicant's reasoning.

The enigma of police officers practising deception to support proceedings in a criminal justice system is challenging for some commentators and indeed some fellow officers. Adherence to necessity tests will confirm that no other option exists for discovering information vital to your investigations. As with all investigative techniques, covert activities are one element of your investigator's armoury to be used when appropriate.

COVERT METHODS 143

SUMMARY OF KEY CONCEPTS

This chapter presents covert options available to you as an investigator. The content equips you to:

- produce applications addressing necessity criteria when seeking authority to deploy covert methodology;

- measure the proportionality of your proposed actions;

- discriminate between witnesses, members of the public and covert human intelligence sources;

- summarise the differences between directed and intrusive surveillance;

- plan your activities to minimise collateral intrusion.

CHECK YOUR KNOWLEDGE

1. You are on duty when you receive information about a suspicious bag hidden in bushes in the local park. You discover this contains clothing from a nearby store. Attached tags suggest the clothing has been stolen. You decide to hide and observe the bag for a short time with a view to identifying the offenders should they return. Does this amount to directed surveillance?

2. While patrolling you are approached by a person. They confide their suspicions about one of their neighbours to you. They believe the neighbour is supplying controlled drugs. They receive a lot of visitors who only stay a short time. Exchange of small packages for money has been observed. Do you consider this person a covert human intelligence source?

3. You identify an opportunity to approach a 15 year-old who you believe will supply information about the activities of their parents who are suspected of involvement in crime. Is this appropriate?

4. You are conducting an operation where a correctly authorised listening device has been installed in a private car. You become aware that the device is recording telephone conversations through the vehicle 'hands-free' system. Does this constitute an interception of communications?

Sample answers to these questions are provided at the end of the book.

FURTHER READING

Ball, K, Haggerty, K D and Lyon, D (2012) *Routledge Handbook of Surveillance Studies*. Abingdon: Routledge.
This collection of essays examines theory and ethics relating to a variety of surveillance forms.

Home Office (2018) *Covert Human Intelligence Sources: Revised Code of Practice*. [online] Available at: https://assets.publishing.service.gov.uk/government/uploads/system/uploads/attachment_data/file/742042/20180802_CHIS_code_.pdf (accessed 12 November 2021).

Home Office (2018) *Covert Surveillance and Property Interference. Revised Code of Practice*. [online] Available at: https://assets.publishing.service.gov.uk/government/uploads/system/uploads/attachment_data/file/742041/201800802_CSPI_code.pdf (accessed 12 November 2021).
These two codes of practice contain helpful examples to assist your understanding.

CHAPTER 8
COMPLEX CASES

LEARNING OBJECTIVES

AFTER READING THIS CHAPTER YOU WILL BE ABLE TO:

- predict events with the potential to become critical incidents;
- prepare a criticality scoring matrix;
- design investigative communication strategies;
- prepare media strategies.

INTRODUCTION

Having read up to this point you may feel that all investigations are complex. 'Major', 'serious', 'organised' or 'complex' are ways of describing offences which, in 2018, the then Home Secretary Sajid Javid described as the most serious threat to the national security of the UK. However, it is important to note that complex crimes are not necessarily organised, which is something many investigators will relate to when dealing with unplanned and reactionary homicides.

Complex enquiries arise from both proactive and reactive approaches; for example, lengthy intelligence-led enquiries into organised crime and reactionary investigations into significant events can both be thought of as complex. In common with much offending, complex crime targets vulnerabilities (social, human, system and commercially based); understanding contributions to these vulnerabilities will prove beneficial to you as the investigator.

Your first experiences of complex investigations will probably be as the initial attending officer to a serious event. No matter how complex, the early stages to any investigation will be supported by the application of good decision making and the golden hour principles (see Chapter 2).

Although serious offences are defined through legislation, section 2(2) of the Powers of Criminal Courts (Sentencing) Act 2000 refers to a series of specified offences. Examining critical incidents supports the conclusion that the context is as important as the categorisation of the offence. It is unlikely that a serious event will be addressed through a triage system such as the Volume Crime Management Model (explored in Chapter 1). Complex crimes will attract a level of resourcing unavailable to the volume crime investigator. Subsequent decision making and strategy development are what sets complex enquiries apart from their more regularly encountered counterparts. This chapter addresses critical incidents, communications strategies and media engagement as a means of introducing you to the complexities of more intricate investigations. The next reflective practice activity asks you to consider how the seriousness of the crime influences the response, before engaging with strategies designed for serious crimes.

REFLECTIVE PRACTICE 8.1

LEVEL 5

Position yourself as a crime investigator in a predominantly rural environment. Let's make it one Iain Stainton is familiar with, the English Lake District. You receive a report of theft of camping equipment from an unattended motor vehicle, the vehicle having been parked in a layby on a remote pass while the owners spent the day fell walking. No CCTV is available, no witnesses are available, the stolen items are not particularly identifiable. In accordance with the Volume Crime Management Model (see Chapter 1) it is probable the incident will be screened, and no further investigation will take place. Now imagine the same car in the same place at the same time on the same day. The difference being that as a patrolling officer you check the vehicle due to a series of thefts from such vehicles in your area, notice suspicious marks on the seats and subsequently discover a dead body in the boot. The area is the same, the available material is the same, the proportional response very different.

Compare the two situations. What can you learn from the response to the more serious incident that can be translated to your dealings with the detection and prevention of volume crimes?

CRITICAL INCIDENTS

Although they are often associated with major investigations, critical incidents can in fact arise from any event. A critical incident is defined as *'any incident where the effectiveness of the police response is likely to have a significant impact on the confidence of the victim, their family and/or the community'* (College of Policing, 2021c, p 1). Originating from the same Macpherson report (1999) which led to encouragement to consider victim-centric practice (see Chapters 4 and 9), critical incident management is strongly linked to decision making, a theme that runs throughout Alison and Crego's (2008) study of such events. The College of Policing (2021c) split critical incident management into four key elements:

1. effectiveness;

2. significant impact;

3. confidence;

4. likelihood.

Effectiveness represents your investigative approach and decision making. The significance of impact will be contextual (see the below critical thinking activity), and the component parts of victim, family and community will include all actors, which may be widespread and should be assessed individually. Confidence applies to both short- and long-term effects and must be addressed contextually as differing communities will have different expectations. The likelihood calculation will draw on a range of factors represented by criticality issues, which will be introduced shortly.

A single critical incident has the potential to have a continuing effect on police–community relations; reverberations from the mishandling of the Stephen Lawrence murder enquiry continue today. As the aftereffects continue, heightened perceptions of vulnerability may occur among the public in the form of a moral panic, as defined by Cohen (2002). An understanding of these societal disciplines will be helpful to you when forecasting the potential of an event becoming a critical incident.

Her Majesty's Inspectorate of Constabulary and Fire & Rescue Services' survey *Public Perceptions of Policing in England and Wales* (HMICFRS, 2018) revealed that 61 per cent of respondents were satisfied with their local police force, rising to 75 per cent effectiveness in dealing with emergencies. While admirable, these figures suggest at least a quarter of those surveyed are not satisfied. Critical incidents can be related to crime, disorder or anti-social behaviour; this chapter follows the book's theme and concentrates on crime.

The College of Policing (2021c) make the valid point that the National Decision Model (see Chapter 3 for details) should be at the centre of your approach to managing critical incidents. A critical incident is not necessarily a serious incident, as outwardly innocuous events may meet the criteria of having a significant impact, as outlined in the below critical thinking activity. To borrow from the golden hour principles (Chapter 2), information may be limited in the initial stages when you are considering whether a situation should be graded as critical. To assist your decision making, the College of Policing (2021c) recommend a criticality matrix based on findings that certain features occur in critical incidents. Table 8.1 shows a suggested scoring matrix based on these factors. You can add or remove column suggestions to cater for the contextual influence of specific circumstances. Use the categories of high, medium or low risk to populate the matrix, providing an objective indication of the situation you are dealing with.

COMPLEX CASES

Table 8.1 Criticality scoring matrix

	Death/ serious injury	Repeat offence	Prominent victim/ offender/ location	Number of victims	Investigative failings	Media interest	Community issues	Police involvement (victim offender)
Victim								
Family								
Community								

Essentially a risk management process, you should identify and analyse threats and vulnerabilities arising from your critical incident before designing a plan based on the predicted impact to mitigate the risk. However, remember that it is virtually impossible to remove risk. A successful assessment includes your acceptable risk threshold. Figure 8.1 illustrates how such an assessment may be calculated. Your risk assessment is an organic calculation and should be regularly reviewed as the context and contributing factors alter.

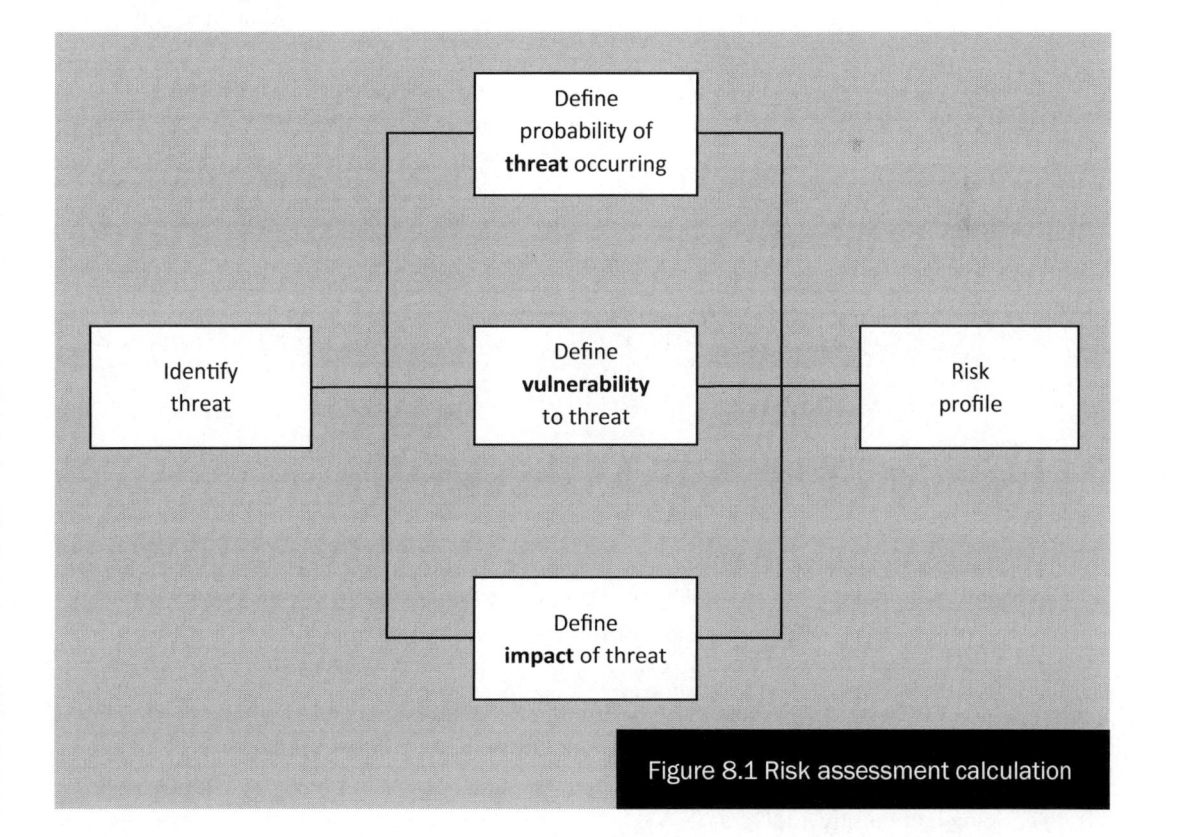

Figure 8.1 Risk assessment calculation

Development, such as your engagement with this book, equips you to prepare to manage critical incidents. Encouragement to reflect on your practice creates a cyclical never-ending process which will assist you in maintaining public confidence throughout your career.

Any officer can nominate a situation as being a potential critical incident, although only senior officers of inspector rank and above can declare one. PIP4 investigators, as defined in Chapter 1, are equipped to offer guidance and advice particularly on management of large-scale critical incidents. Enquiries and reports, such as those referred to in Chapter 9, represent transparency and accountability of investigative practice in action and should be viewed as contributing to the maintenance of confidence in association with the way you deal with critical incidents. Where the potential for community impact has been recognised, this must be addressed. Community impact assessments facilitate this and will be explained next.

CRITICAL THINKING ACTIVITY 8.1

LEVEL 5

Imagine a situation where in your policing role you are directed to attend a report of a window being smashed at a residential address, a relatively minor offence. While travelling to the scene you are informed that a crowd is gathering outside the address. An intelligence check reveals the occupant to be a convicted offender who is subject to a sexual harm prevention order.

Do you believe this meets the criteria for a critical incident? Evaluate the above and design a response to meet the needs of the situation.

COMMUNITY IMPACT ASSESSMENTS

The purpose of a community impact assessment (CIA) is to identify issues that affect a community's confidence in the ability of the police to respond effectively to their needs. (College of Policing, 2020a). Inclusive of the wider community, Innes (2010) makes the point that people who are not otherwise affected by the crime itself may experience fear and anxiety as a result of its occurrence. CIAs are effectively a larger-scale risk assessment, and their aim is to enhance understanding of impact factors, identify vulnerable individuals and groups, and provide assessment of community confidence while developing community intelligence.

An impact assessment should include:

- details of incident or planned action;
- location;
- affected communities/groups;
- community characteristics;
- specific individuals or groups affected;
- existing tensions;
- partner agencies;
- potential impact;
- risk factors;
- response factors/action plan.

When threats and vulnerabilities have been identified, you are then in a position to mitigate the threat either by action or through engagement with other agencies or organisations. The nature of criminal investigation sees events on the edge of societal norms becoming the focus of action. This action will affect a variety of individuals and communities. Any visit to social media confirms the wide variety of opinions as to any organisation's action or perceived lack of action. Critical incidents and associated assessments are one way of addressing this to maintain trust and community cohesion.

Critical incident management and community impact assessments are dependent upon strong communication strategies. Media engagement represents one of the most efficient forms of communication. Communications and media strategies will now be explored in more depth.

EVIDENCE-BASED POLICING

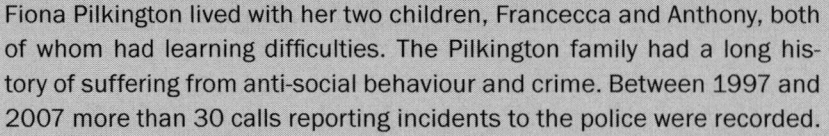

Fiona Pilkington lived with her two children, Francecca and Anthony, both of whom had learning difficulties. The Pilkington family had a long history of suffering from anti-social behaviour and crime. Between 1997 and 2007 more than 30 calls reporting incidents to the police were recorded.

The Independent Police Complaints Commission report (2009), which followed the events of 23 October 2007 when Fiona killed herself and Francecca, found a series of repeated police failings to recognise the combined impact of the targeting of the family and the stress of her family background; the situation was intolerable for the vulnerable household. As discussed, critical incidents may not be dramatic in themselves. Having an understanding of the issues that may be experienced by individuals or communities in considering whether an incident is critical is indicative of a professional problem-solving approach to incidents you will be called to deal with.

COMMUNICATIONS STRATEGY

Communications are a core element of an investigator's skillset. Victims, witnesses, members of the public, colleagues and journalists all want to know what is happening and what you plan to do. Chapter 2 introduced the IIMARCH briefing model and this section expands on this, as well as outlining the alternative SAFCOM model while detailing strategic communication deliberations.

The individualistic detective beloved of popular drama is the antithesis of the modern investigator. The ability to maintain internal communications with colleagues, specialists and subsequently the wide variety of personnel you will encounter in the criminal justice system, and externally through both multi-agency and community needs, demands an informed approach to communicating. The Yorkshire Ripper enquiry described in Chapters 3 and 9 highlights the challenges caused by poor communication. Sutcliffe was interviewed numerous times during the enquiry, and internal communications failed to make adequate links. Contrast this with the 2006 arrest of Steve Wright for the murders of five women in Ipswich spanning a period of two months. Lessons learnt from the 1980s resulted in an evidence-led structured enquiry as opposed to the earlier investigation where reactions to new material led to existing lines of enquiry being abandoned before they concluded.

Communications can be separated into two component parts: internal and external. Internal communications can range from a colleague's first question on arrival at a crime scene, 'what happened?', to pre-trial discussions with counsel. External communications can range from multi-agency enquiries to engagement with community groups. This chapter will now look at each of these parts in turn.

INTERNAL COMMUNICATIONS

Internal communications refer to communication strategies within the investigative organisation. These include making colleagues aware of your lines of enquiry in the hope they can assist and briefing specialists or senior colleagues about the current situation. Chapter 7 refers to authorisation levels for covert deployments, and such briefings form part of these internal communications.

One of the most common forms of internal communications are identifications. Images from CCTV often include offenders or witnesses; the next step involves identifying the person from the picture. This type of internal communication is the ideal example. Such an appeal is recognised as good practice when you have an image but do not have a name. Colleagues represent a good chance of resolving the issue while maintaining credibility of evidence. Code D of the Police and Criminal Evidence Act 1984 provides the guidance as to how to do this legally, combining legislation and effective enquiries in one specific line of enquiry. Such communications extend to internally publicising specific elements of the offence you are investigating where you believe your fellow investigators may be able to assist. It is noteworthy that this extends to post arrest. Publicising identifiable aspects of the modus operandi may assist colleagues to make links between offenders and events. Communications should use the most effective means, for example briefings, intranet, email or posters. Where the communications are specific to an enquiry, as in the child murder policing spotlight which follows, and timeliness is of the essence, in person or virtual briefings are among the most effective.

The Home Office (2020) recommend the IIMARCH briefing model (outlined in Chapter 2), and this is without doubt an effective briefing model. We will however draw your attention to the SAFCOM model (College of Policing, 2021b), which you may prefer as a foundation for more dynamic briefings.

- **S**ituation. Explain what has given rise to your briefing. Plan on the basis that your audience does not know: remember to never assume they do have prior knowledge.

- **A**im. What are you hoping to achieve? An aim represents your overall intent; objectives are the steps you will take to achieve your aim.

- **F**actors. This is the point for your assessments. What risks or threats have you identified, how will you address them, and what do you need to achieve your aims?

- **C**hoices. What are the options for solving the problem?

- **O**ptions. Which is your preferred option and why?

- **M**onitoring. The point that these are fast-moving organic situations has already been made. Re-enforce this with a plan for monitoring to see if your response continues to be valid in a changing environment.

You will probably have noticed similarities with the National Decision Model (NDM), from Chapter 3. This model provides a good companion to the NDM, allowing you to demonstrate your grasp and understanding to others in a way that encourages brevity, accuracy and speed.

POLICING SPOTLIGHT

As a member of the investigation team in an early 2000s murder investigation of a young child, I (Iain Stainton) continue to be influenced by the briefing styles used throughout the enquiry.

This multi-agency enquiry was highly emotive as a young child battled for his life while family members were identified as suspects.

The senior investigating officer (SIO) ensured that each day started and finished with a briefing. These were inclusive and all members of the team were invited; you knew what was happening throughout all strands of the enquiry. Conducted by the SIO, teams could contribute their elements of the investigation and compare findings with others in a collegiate atmosphere. The SIO ensured all agencies were included in these often-candid exchanges. Time was made to discuss and integrate information, so all enquiry officers were constantly included by name throughout, ensuring all team members felt invested in the whole enquiry.

Any enquiry teams unable to attend were encouraged to contribute their findings, thoughts and suspicions remotely.

Nearly 20 years later, these arrangements remain entrenched in my memory as 'best practice'.

The influence of making time and valuing these briefings spread to every aspect of this wide-ranging investigation, which in spite of the emotional content remains positively entrenched in my memory.

CRITICAL THINKING ACTIVITY 8.2

LEVEL 4

No matter your level of experience, you will be an expert at presentations. This may be as a result of delivering many of them but is more likely to result from your experience of being presented to. Throughout school, college and employment, you have sat through good and poor presentations. Subject expertise is no guarantee of presentational ability. The best of messages gets lost when the presentation does not engage your attention.

Take a moment to reflect on presentations or briefings you have experienced or endured. Draw positives from those that worked best and identify negatives from others. Compile these traits and try to implant them in your future briefings.

EXTERNAL COMMUNICATIONS

Much of the success of an investigation is dependent upon communications, and Chapter 6 describes an assortment of sources of assistance. The inability to initiate and receive information would be a significant hurdle to the smooth running of your investigations, and the requirement for widening your communications outside the realm of investigators occurs more often than you think. The majority of your investigations originate from events occurring in public; the general public's interest in crime is recognised in Chapter 1. External communications are dependent on framing your message to maximise the appeal or message of reassurance. When issuing your message, be aware that some information is already public. Do not contradict information your audience already possess unless you need to counter false material. Identify communication responsibilities because constantly changing the 'faces of the investigation' does not create a good impression. Make sure the point of contact is comfortable and capable of undertaking the task. If your enquiry involves multiple agencies, establish an agreed protocol to ensure a consistency of message. Presenters often refer to 'knowing your audience', which refers to tailoring your communications to the intended audience. You will find that you are already experienced in this; for example, imagine how you might moderate your conversation with a traumatised person differently compared to conversation with a close friend during a social occasion.

If you are sharing material among agencies, you should develop a memorandum of understanding detailing whether any further distribution is possible and how the material should be treated. Assumptions lead to difficult conversations when they are proved wrong. You should plan for your strategies to complement each other, as an interview strategy can be undermined by a media or house-to-house strategy that releases information about an offence you want to retain for future interviews.

External communications involve transmitting messages to a diverse collection of cultures and communities. This complex structure introduces communication challenges of its own before the impact of crime and vulnerability is catered for. Storytelling has long been relied upon for communicating information and learning. Value and trust are associated with storytelling, thus establishing mutual understanding in dynamic environments. Cooren (2000) suggests that using storytelling to relay content and context leads to effective interpretation and subsequent action. The SAFCOM model outlined earlier lends itself to such an approach, which is worthy of consideration.

At this point in time, it is right to add social media to the lexicon of communications available to investigators. Concentrating on Facebook and Twitter, police social media presence features force-level and departmental accounts. Recent monitoring suggests these concentrate on recruitment, proactive crime prevention messaging, missing persons, campaigns and 'press releases' about notable incidents. Departmental and local area accounts spread messages of good practice, community liaison events, traffic news and local crime updates and appeals; a sub-sector of accounts concentrate on arrests, while accounts on traffic enforcement function as a deterrent. A move towards subscription newsletters has been noted on local social media accounts. Social media communication lends itself to crisis situations; in chaotic and confusing environments, it is critical to get the correct messages to the maximum amount of people and to address the information vacuum, which is likely to be filled with rumour and innuendo. For example, social media was used to distribute advice and information during the 2017 Manchester Arena attack, and it was described as having a considerable influence on situational awareness and the general intelligence picture by the Kerslake Report (2018).

Media engagement represents one of your most effective forms of communication, allowing your message to reach a range of people in a way no other option will. The next section will explore this aspect of investigation.

MEDIA ENGAGEMENT

Feist (1999) explains that media handling in serious crime investigations is a complex issue. It varies between providing access to the public and generating information to misleading information interfering with the legal process. Media strategies are a critical skill and Adhami and Browne (1996) outline how media strategies:

- acquire information;

- manage interest to avoid misinformation and interference;

- provide accurate information;

- minimise societal concerns over fear of crime;

- disseminate appropriate advice;

- reinforce reputational issues.

Investigators are rightly concerned with events and investigative progress; the media follow a newsworthiness criterion, selecting the most newsworthy material on behalf of the public. The reporting of serious crime continues to be disproportionate to its statistical occurrence (Ditton and Duffy, 1983), inadvertently creating disproportionate fears among communities. The dominant partner in the investigator–media relationship can be recognised from Crandon and Dunne's 1997 research, which discovered that in excess of 90 per cent of interactions were initiated by the police.

Feist (1999) outlines what aspects a selection of senior investigators consider contributes to newsworthiness:

- age, background of victim;

- severity of offence;

- location;

- prevalence of similar, linked offences.

This is not an exhaustive list but merely a guide based on experience. An understanding of what will prove attractive in the competitive news environment can be gained through communications specialists. Communications departments should be an inherent part of the investigator's armoury. Specialists in media and communications are as valuable as any other investigative specialist, arguably more so when the public reach of the media is brought into the equation.

It is accepted that to generate interest and material through a media strategy there will be a requirement to provide information. This must be supplied in accordance with Criminal Procedure and Investigations Act 1996 and Contempt of Court Act 1981. The dangers of inappropriate information exchanges are illustrated by the 2011 investigation into the murders of Sian O'Callaghan and Becky Godden-Edwards, where the relationship between the senior investigating officer and media contributed to not guilty directions in respect of the murder of Godden-Edwards and subsequent dismissal of Detective Superintendent Fulcher.

The 2012 Leveson enquiry and the case of *Sir Cliff Richard v BBC and Chief Constable of South Yorkshire Police* [2018] EWHC 1837 focused on the relationship between the police and press, giving rise to the College of Policing's 2016 guidance on maintaining professional relationships.

The manner of the relationship can influence the tone of reporting, which has the potential to influence how the material is digested within a community. The headline '1 in 5 British Muslims have sympathy for ISIS' (*The Sun*, 2015) was subsequently proven to be misleading reporting of a survey, a practice referred to as 'clickbait' in social media circles.

The dangers of journalists' parallel investigations contaminating evidence trails is demonstrated in the 1994 investigation into the activities of Fred and Rose West, where substantial newspaper financial inducements to witnesses to share their stories affected the credibility of subsequent evidence – a situation neatly summarised by West's entreaties to his son to sell his story and make as much as he could.

More complex media engagement arises from a 'profiling' (Chapter 3) aspect where appeals and briefings are tailored to exert pressure and exploit the moral sensibilities of offenders or witnesses.

Mawby (1999) argues that the current media environment is less easy to control. The rise of citizen journalism where members of the public upload events, simultaneously creating a watchdog environment, contributes to the challenging situation. Innes (1999) elaborates that communication developments have altered societal understandings. Combining the reach of mass communication, social media and fictionalised drama results in a degree of knowledge about issues the majority will never experience. This is prevalent in the investigative arena, being particularly noticeable where interaction with the general public is sought.

POLICING SPOTLIGHT

As an academic with policing experience, I (Iain Stainton) often have the opportunity to comment on policing matters through the media. The breadth of matters policing can be involved in is huge. The range of topics and demands on the police to satisfy public expectations can be illustrated in a two-day period when my media engagement ranged from commenting on a terrorist atrocity, a child abduction case, to young children who had been admonished for picking flowers from the roadside as a present for Mother's Day. The public-facing demands of investigation are not restricted to senior officers. The 24/7 rolling news and social media era has resulted in a range of officers finding themselves managing media engagement. You are used to discussing all manner of things with members of the public; you can bring these communication skills to the wider audience media allows.

REFLECTIVE PRACTICE 8.2

LEVEL 6

Put yourself in the position of a case officer who is due to make a media appearance following a burglary where the elderly householder disturbed the offenders. You want to provide reassurance, update the public and appeal for information. In accordance with most media appearances, you will have no more than two minutes to do this. Evaluate this situation and consider the following questions.

How will you plan your appeal? How would you then deal with a line of questioning based on two similar offences in the area in the recent past?

CONCLUSION

You will have identified the theme of communication throughout this chapter. Complex investigations are dependent upon enhanced communication techniques throughout. It is worth mentioning that this includes listening and reading alongside speaking and writing. The challenge of complexity rises alongside the number of people involved. As an investigator you are supported by a huge team (over 150,000 officers without including other specialists or agencies). As with all complex issues, the management of this is paramount. The experiences and lessons you gain in the early stages of your career will provide an ideal foundation for the senior stages.

Experience is not based on how long you have been doing the job. You will encounter people that have been doing the same thing with little or no development for many years; conversely, others with a shorter time scale in the position will have reviewed, reflected and developed their knowledge and understanding – this is the experience to be respected.

SUMMARY OF KEY CONCEPTS

This chapter highlighted complex enquiries, in particular critical incidents and communication strategies. The content enables you to:

- approach complex issues with confidence;
- assess events to differentiate those with the potential to undermine confidence in policing;
- organise media support to your practice;
- compose briefings.

CHECK YOUR KNOWLEDGE

1. Fill in the blanks:

    A critical incident can be defined as .... incident where the effectiveness of the police response is .... to have a significant impact on the .... of the victim, their family and/or the ....

2. Identify the first step of a risk assessment.

3. Critical incident guidance arose from which enquiry report?

4. Communications strategies can be divided into which two components?

Sample answers to these questions are provided at the end of the book.

FURTHER READING

Alison, L and Crego, J (2008) *Policing Critical Incidents*. Cullompton: Willan. Drawing on real-world events, this book provides an ideal source of further information on managing critical incidents.

The College of Policing Authorised Professional Practice web resources provide the latest thinking and guidance on your chosen areas of investigative practice. These are available at: www.app.college.police.uk

CHAPTER 9
MEASURING INVESTIGATIVE SUCCESS

LEARNING OBJECTIVES

AFTER READING THIS CHAPTER YOU WILL BE ABLE TO:

- evaluate measures of investigative success;
- summarise enquiry reports;
- outline police complaints and discipline guidelines;
- identify Criminal Procedure and Investigations Act disclosure requirements.

INTRODUCTION

Chapter 1 started with reference to fictional detectives, working on one case at a time, always solving the crime through a mixture of intuition and intelligence. To return to the jigsaw analogy of Chapter 2, it is as if they are assembling pieces having already seen the finished puzzle, magically highlighting their prowess as a puzzler. This represents the public's views of investigative practice, magical and mysterious. The next influencer of opinion is provided by high-profile cases and enquiries revealing poor practice. Recognising perceptions and how they are created allows you to play your part in creating a real-world impression through your own professional practice.

Society places trust in investigators to reactively and proactively address a diverse range of issues identified as undesirable by the public. This places investigators in a situation investigating breaches of acceptable behaviour while operating in an acceptable manner: a challenging situation for any person.

Investigative failures leading to wrongful convictions or failed prosecutions adversely impact public confidence, creating a cyclical process where lack of confidence in police impacts on crime, crime reporting and public engagement with the investigative process.

The portrayal of fictional detectives solving crimes with unlimited and unrealistic resources which features daily in the media creates a public expectation of offenders being caught and punished every time, in a very short space of time. This is a situation Tyler (2005) named the 'Hollywood effect'. This chapter will examine how investigative success is measured, detail how enquiries originating from investigative failures influence future practice before addressing complaints made about practice. The chapter concludes by looking at one of the most contentious areas: that of disclosure. We begin with a reflective practice activity.

REFLECTIVE PRACTICE 9.1

LEVEL 6

As a policing student, you have adopted a critical learning approach to investigation. Take a moment to contemplate what initially drew you to criminal investigation. Compare your original inspiration to your current opinions and then assess which factors have led to this. Your conclusion will identify how you can continue your professional development as an investigator.

This activity will enable you to identify what is important to the people you will encounter as a detective.

INVESTIGATIVE SUCCESS?

Failure attracts more exposure than success. The reverberations of enquiries such as Byford (1981), Macpherson (1999) and Bichard (2004) continue to influence practice within and opinion outside policing. This chapter includes commentary on such reports. Successful investigations tend to attract some media comment at the conclusion of any trial but rarely result in reflections to the depth of these reports. This leads to the question of what constitutes a successful investigation. Convictions, statistics, complaints and evaluations will be examined in an attempt to answer the question.

STATISTICS

Chapter 1 examined crime statistics and the many variables impacting on what and how crimes are recorded. For example, consider the following scenarios.

- A victim reports a course of offending conduct involving multiple events: one crime will be recorded. If they report each event separately, multiple crimes will be recorded.

- A crime is recorded as finished (detected) when a suspect is charged, reported or cautioned. If a subsequent trial finds them to be not guilty, the statistics will continue to record that crime as detected.

- Fraud offences collated nationally.

- Serious events such as murder amount to one crime as would a minor theft, the operational demands being very different.

Discrepancies between the Telephone-operated Crime Survey for England and Wales (TCSEW) and police recorded crime can be explained by the fact that crimes which are not reported or recorded by the police may feature in the TCSEW. Additionally, many crimes will be unreported to either survey. O'Neill (2018) suggests that success measured through recorded detections may be subject to perverse incentives. There is a perceived encouragement to manipulate statistics by concentrating on more detectable offences at the expense of harder-to-solve offences.

Questionable recording approaches, as described in some Her Majesty's Inspectorate of Constabulary and Fire & Rescue Services' Police Effectiveness, Efficiency and Legitimacy

(PEEL) inspections of police forces (HMICFRS, 2018, 2019) and discussed in the forthcoming evaluation section, contribute to confirming Strathern's (1997, p 308) assertion that *'when a measure becomes a target, it ceases to be a good measure'*.

CONVICTIONS

Brookman and Innes' (2013) statement that *'detective culture is largely predicted upon catching bad guys'* suggests that this traditional indicator of investigative success is also subject to many variables. As evidenced in the policing spotlight on the 2010 Cumbria shootings (see Chapter 2), a great deal of time and resources can be spent on matters which will never result in a court appearance. This is emphasised on a national basis by the origins of the 2012 Operation Yewtree investigation. Any officer with experience of the criminal justice system will take exception to Eck and Rossmo's (2019) submission that a crime can only be solved through evidence, and therefore unsolved or incorrectly solved crimes must be due to evidential failures or substandard evidence collection, evaluation or analysis. There are many aspects of a finding of guilt that you are unable to control, such as witness accounts in court or jury perception. Investigative failings may not be the prime motivator of a not guilty verdict.

EVIDENCE-BASED POLICING

The risks of measuring success by statistics are underlined by Gill's 1987 article, which examined the reliability of police crime detection figures, following an exposure by the *Observer* newspaper in 1986 that officers had been processing admissions from convicted criminals who could not have committed the offences they confessed to. At the time, crimes may have been classed as detected where evidence pointing to an offender existed but the circumstances allowed no further action to be taken. One such circumstance was when a convicted offender was serving a custodial sentence and admitted their part in further offences but no further action could be authorised where it was believed no additional sentence would be forthcoming. In some forces, more than 50 per cent of the detection rate could be attributed to this method of 'clearing up' crimes. Rising crime rates, targets and the requirement to demonstrate success all contributed to this questionable practice where confessions were accepted with little or no confirmatory enquiries becoming commonplace in some force areas. Gill suggests that time spent on statistical manipulation to provide an aura of success took place at the expense of actually investigating crime. This is a premise confirmed by the decrease in detection rates following updated guidance which resulted in the virtual elimination of the practice.

EVALUATIONS

Her Majesty's Inspectorate of Constabulary and Fire & Rescue Services (HMICFRS) conduct annual inspections of police forces in England and Wales, and the assessments of Police Effectiveness, Efficiency and Legitimacy (PEEL) are based on the following themes or pillars of operation:

- crime recording;

- preventing and deterring crime and anti-social behaviour;

- responding to the public;

- investigating crime;

- protecting vulnerable people;

- managing offenders;

- serious and organised crime;

- strategic/specialist capabilities.

Investigations are sampled, officers spoken to and policy and procedure examined. This mixed-method, quantitative/qualitative approach may include areas of contemporary pressure to contribute to a timely recognition of practice before grading performance and making recommendations. It is important to remember that PEEL assessments are broadly supported by the police and public (Ipsos, 2015). The following critical thinking activity places you in a position to represent both the police and public, confirming Sir Robert Peel's (1829) view that the police are the public and the public are the police.

CRITICAL THINKING ACTIVITY 9.1

LEVEL 5

Assess the following measures of investigative success in order from least to most important to you:

- identifying suspects;

- successful prosecution;

- guilty plea;

- victim satisfaction;

- self-satisfaction;

- reduced crime levels;

- awards, commendations;

- procedural compliant.

Now analyse why you categorised them as you did. This will allow you to recognise what is important to you about the investigative function.

Neyroud and Beckley (2001) state that *'a shift from a control paradigm to a learning paradigm that values risk taking and experimentation may result in long term solutions to problems that equip police officers to face emerging... issues'*. This links to the College of Policing's drive for evidence-based policing and developments, such as the National Decision Model (College of Policing, 2013b).

HMICFRS also produce reports into specific areas of policing, such as public order, cyber-crime and sexual offences. These focused reports represent a more proactive stance than reports into policing commissioned by the government following events or investigations. A sample of reports will now be scrutinised to stress how identified poor practice often leads to change, as asserted by Neyroud and Beckley's (2001) vicious cycle (see Chapter 1).

REPORTS

This section examines a selection of key reports arising from and influencing investigative practice and will highlight the contribution these and other similar enquiries have made to investigative practice.

THE SCARMAN REPORT

The Scarman report (1981) was commissioned by the Home Office following a series of riots which took place across England in the summer of 1981. Liverpool, Manchester, Leeds and Birmingham all experienced large-scale disorder, although the report concentrated on the Brixton riots. Scarman found that a complicated set of political, social and economic factors contributed to the violence, although the report is remembered for its identification of the disproportionate use of stop and search powers, which served to further alienate the predominantly black local population. Changes to practice, training and police recruitment were recommended, and the report led to the safeguards found within the Police and Criminal Evidence Act 1984 (PACE). Most officers would agree that this represents one of the most significant pieces of legislation in policing in recent history. Police discipline codes, which are presented later in this chapter, were amended alongside the introduction of community liaison. These are all factors which continue to this day.

ROYAL COMMISSION ON CRIMINAL JUSTICE

The realisation that the evolution of law and policy had become piecemeal by the early 1980s led to the Royal Commission on Criminal Justice report (1981). The situation can be illustrated by the case of Maxwell Confait, who was murdered in 1972. The investigation and subsequent trial are infamous for the use of false confessions and manipulative investigative practice. The original findings of guilt against the three accused were subsequently overturned by the Court of Appeal finding a miscarriage of justice had occurred. The Royal Commission examined the balance between powers and rights. This scrutiny of rights such as silence, detention periods and interview procedures joins the Scarman report in influencing the content of PACE. The creation of an independent prosecution in the form of the Crown Prosecution Service (CPS) transformed the then predominant situation where the investigators themselves in the form of the police led prosecutions

THE BYFORD REPORT

Forty years after his arrest, the crimes of Peter Sutcliffe (otherwise known as the Yorkshire Ripper) continue to resonate with the public in a way few other investigations can match. Sutcliffe was found guilty of the murder of 13 women and attempted murder of seven during a five-year period. The impact these killings had on society cannot be underestimated. A culture of fear led to a moral panic rarely matched in modern times. Following his conviction, a report into the conduct of the investigation was commissioned by the Home Secretary. The Byford report was completed in 1981, although the papers were not made publicly available until 2006. The report found that significant errors of judgement predominated the enquiry. In these pre-computer times, the incident room was ill prepared to deal with an investigation of its size, and its operation was described as ineffective. Suggestions of investigative bias, misogyny and sexist attitudes affecting decision making are associated with this influential investigation (Smith, 1993; Wattis, 2018). Iain Stainton was a junior officer at the time of Sutcliffe's arrest, and reflective practice activity 9.2 is based on his later involvement with this infamous killer.

In a precursor to *Commissioner of Police of the Metropolis (Appellant) v DSD and another (Respondents)* [2018] UKSC 11 on appeal from [2015] EWCA Civ 646 (discussed in Chapter 3), relatives of Sutcliffe's final victim initiated legal action against West Yorkshire Police. They alleged that a failure to trace Sutcliffe represented a breakdown of a duty of care, which directly led to the death of Jacqueline Hill. The court found that no direct link could be established; however, this situation was amended some years later by the above DSD case. The Byford report gave rise to Major Incident Room Standardised Administrative Procedures (MIRSAP), which provide guidance on all aspects of creating and running a major incident room. The computerisation of records led to the Home Office Large Major Enquiry System (HOLMES), version 2 of which supports large-scale enquiries to this day. Training and registration of senior investigating officers (SIOs), specialist support and media liaison were all influenced by this wide-ranging report.

REFLECTIVE PRACTICE 9.2

LEVEL 5

In 2005, Peter Sutcliffe was authorised to be escorted from Broadmoor high-security psychiatric hospital to visit Arnside, Cumbria, where his father's ashes had been scattered. The visit, which was revealed by the media shortly afterwards, generated much national and local comment. I (Iain Stainton) had responsibility for planning and conducting the local element and retain clear memories of the day.

Imagine you were placed in a similar position and consider the following questions. How would you devise a plan and prepare for any ramifications? How would you construct your decision making and approach to ensure the safety of a subject with such an offending history?

THE MACPHERSON REPORT

Described as a watershed in the history of policing (Lawrence, 2009), the Macpherson report (1999) was the result of a public enquiry into the investigation into the death of Stephen Lawrence. Best known for the finding of 'institutional racism', the enquiry made 70 recommendations ranging from the abolition of the common law double jeopardy rule, meaning that a person could not be tried twice for the same offence, to the requirement to ensure police officers are first aid trained. The Macpherson report continues to influence investigative practice.

Stephen Lawrence was murdered in 1993, and despite two investigations into the events, widespread publicity and arrests, no suspects appeared in court until 2012 when forensic analysis, unavailable earlier, led to the convictions of Gary Dobson and David Norris for the murder. Hall et al (2009) suggest that the murder was the most significant event in bringing violent racism to the top of the political and social agenda. The influence of the recommendations is reflected in Table 9.1, summarising enquiries and their influence on policing. Griffiths (2009) submits that the enquiry was so significant he likens the changes to a 'progression of competence model', starting with:

1. unconscious incompetence, where an organisation is unaware of failings;

2. conscious incompetence, where awareness and steps to address this are formulated;

3. conscious competence, where training, discussion and application surround the adoption of improved practices;

4. unconscious competence, where practice is culturally embedded.

This is a model which aligns with your overall progression as an investigator from not knowing what you do not know to the smooth use of previously complicated techniques.

THE PATTEN REPORT

Studying policing practice in extreme environments often leads to suggestions for refining methodology in less testing times (Tomlinson, 2000). Tomlinson (2000, p 103) states that the Patten report on policing in Northern Ireland deserved *'to be read more widely to stimulate debate about the future of policing'*. Described as the most significant and complex blueprint for police reform in the world (Topping, 2008), the 1999 Patten report was officially titled *A New Beginning: Policing in Northern Ireland.* The Report of the Independent Commission on Policing for Northern Ireland accompanied the Belfast

(Good Friday) Agreement, which brought a 30-year period of extreme violence, known as 'The Troubles', to an end. Policing during this period was carried out by the Royal Ulster Constabulary (RUC). The report sought to identify a model of community engagement to move policing forward. Patten recommended a human rights based approach, placing rights at the centre of policing, demilitarising police buildings and vehicles, and establishing strong community and police links. The recommendations extended to not flying union flags from police buildings and developing a policing board to oversee the work of the police. The RUC was reformed as the Police Service of Northern Ireland (PSNI) following the report. Over 6000 personnel make this the third largest force in the United Kingdom. Patten reinforces the requirements for community links and the importance of public-facing aspects of policing.

THE BICHARD REPORT

Enquiries are often associated with tragedy, and Bichard is no exception. Holly Wells and Jessica Chapman, two 10 year-old girls, were murdered in 2002 by Ian Huntley. Huntley was working at the girls' school in Soham and had a history of coming to the attention of the police and social services in connection with young girls, due to allegations of rape, indecent assault and burglary. This contributed to an intelligence picture although none of these incidences had resulted in a conviction. Misunderstandings and failures of practice meant Huntley passed a vetting check where questions should have arisen. The Bichard enquiry investigated the child protection implications of procedures. The misunderstanding of data protection legislation, together with an unsystematic approach, were highlighted as contributing factors, and resulted in the Management of Police Information (MOPI) guidelines.

Table 9.1 provides a summary of these reports and associated developments.

Table 9.1 Enquiries and recommendations

Enquiry/report	Instigation	Summary	Resulted in:
Royal Commission on Criminal Justice report (1981)			CPS
			PACE
			Rights to silence
			Detention periods
			Recorded interviews
Scarman 1981	Brixton Riots	Indiscriminate use of police powers	Police and Criminal Evidence Act 1984 (PACE)
			Police Complaints Authority

Table 9.1 (continued)

Enquiry/report	Instigation	Summary	Resulted in:
Byford 1981	Peter Sutcliffe (Yorkshire Ripper) investigation	Decision making Investigative mindset	Home Office Large Major Enquiry System (HOLMES)
			Major Incident Room Standard Administrative Procedures (MIRSAP)
Macpherson 1999	Murder of Stephen Lawrence	Institutional racism	Defining racist incidents
			Independent inspections
			Victim centring
			Abolition of the double jeopardy rule
			Family liaison officers
			Reviews of investigations
			Review of initial response to major crimes
			Police discipline codes
			Reform of police misconduct enquiries
Patten 1999	Belfast Agreement Policing Northern Ireland		Police Service of Northern Ireland (PSNI)
Bichard 2004	Murders of Holly Wells and Jessica Chapman		Management of Police Information (MOPI) guidelines

ENQUIRY THEMES

The relevance of public enquiries can be evidenced by exploring enquiries such as those outlined in this chapter, resulting in a number of reoccurring themes being identified:

- public engagement;

- victim-centric enquiries;

- decision making;

- misunderstandings;

- education;

- mentality approaches.

Victim and public connection themes are referred to throughout this book and commonly feature throughout policing texts. The importance of your decision making lacking bias and being based on a sound investigative knowledge is acknowledged by the College of Policing's (2013b) commitment that:

> **Decision makers will receive the support of their organisation in instances where it can be shown that their decisions were assessed and managed reasonably in the circumstances existing at the time. This support applies even where harm results from those decisions and actions.**

Decision making and bias is explored in more detail in Chapters 2 and 3. As a reader of this book, you will already recognise the dangers of misunderstandings and benefits of learning, an approach which will benefit your policing career. Often arising from situations occurring on the margins of society, rarely encountered by members of the public, you may find it challenging to correlate these reports with your own reflective practice. You have spent a lifetime reflecting and learning from your experiences, and reflective practice simply involves recoding these reflections in a way to support your learning. Keen observation, reasoning and analysis are personal qualities essential for the reflective practitioner (Dewey, 1910), which coincidentally match the attributes Lefkowitz (2010) identified in research into police officer characteristics. You should view enquiry reports as you would reflective practice: an opportunity to learn from experiences in a manner which matches developments in evidence-based policing.

Enquiries and reports represent independent inspections of policing, a viewpoint which has been criticised in the past where police officers investigated alleged wrongdoings by other officers, a state of affairs which will now be explored.

COMPLAINTS AND ACCOUNTABILITY

Police officers have powers unavailable to others, such as arrest, search and use of force. When dealing with behaviours on the margins of acceptability and making decisions in fast-moving dynamic situations, it is probable that actions will result in grievances. Therefore, an effective mechanism for dealing with complaints is key to maintaining public support. Oversight and accountability are imperative to socially acceptable policing and to maintaining public support. The notion of independence is central to this accountability; the reports referenced above all represent independent examination of investigative failures. The Royal Commission on Criminal Justice led to the implementation of independent prosecution through the establishment of the CPS in answer to a series of miscarriages of justice. This independence provides legitimacy to the process of examining and addressing breakdowns of investigative practice. Such is the importance of this concept that the Independent Office for Police Conduct (IOPC) and its predecessor, the Independent Police Complaints Commission (IPCC), feature the term prominently in their titles.

The role of enquiries in shaping the response to police complaints can be illustrated from the 1962 Royal Commission on Police, which reported that no formal system for dealing with complaints existed, through to Scarman (1981), which identified a lack of public confidence in the complaints systems resulting in the establishment of the Police Complaints Authority, through to the IPCC, which originated from Macpherson (1999).

The House of Commons' briefing paper *Police Complaints and Discipline* (Brown, 2020) describes three actors in the current police complaints system.

1. The IOPC conducts investigations into serious complaint and conduct matters and oversees the complaints system.

2. The police force Professional Standards Departments (PSD) are responsible for investigating most complaints in their own force area.

3. Police and crime commissioners are responsible for monitoring complaints procedures.

While the IOPC does maintain an investigative capability, the majority of complaints are dealt with by police force PSD. The police complaints and discipline regulations centre on proportionate actions (see Chapter 7 for an examination of proportionality) and standards of behaviour, as detailed in Table 9.2.

Table 9.2 Standards of professional behaviour

Schedule 2 The Police (Conduct) Regulations 2020	
Honesty and integrity	Police officers are honest, act with integrity and do not compromise or abuse their position.
Authority, respect and courtesy	Police officers act with self-control and tolerance, treating members of the public and colleagues with respect and courtesy.
	Police officers do not abuse their powers or authority and respect the rights of all individuals.
Equality and diversity	Police officers act with fairness and impartiality. They do not discriminate unlawfully or unfairly.
Use of force	Police officers only use force to the extent that it is necessary, proportionate and reasonable in all the circumstances.
Orders and instructions	Police officers only give and carry out lawful orders and instructions.
	Police officers abide by police regulations, force policies and lawful orders.
Duties and responsibilities	Police officers are diligent in the exercise of their duties and responsibilities.
	Police officers have a responsibility to give appropriate cooperation during investigations, enquiries and formal proceedings, participating openly and professionally in line with the expectations of a police officer when identified as a witness.
Confidentiality	Police officers treat information with respect and access or disclose it only in the proper course of police duties.
Fitness for duty	Police officers when on duty or presenting themselves for duty are fit to carry out their responsibilities.
Discreditable conduct	Police officers behave in a manner which does not discredit the police service or undermine public confidence in it, whether on or off duty.
	Police officers report any action taken against them for a criminal offence, any conditions imposed on them by a court or the receipt of any penalty notice.
Challenging and reporting improper conduct	Police officers report, challenge or take action against the conduct of colleagues which has fallen below the Standards of Professional Behaviour.

The IOPC (2019) report showed that the most common causes for complaints from members of the public involve:

- neglect or failure of duty;
- incivility;
- assault.

In line with evidence-based policing, the IOPC (2020) stress the learning which may be extracted from complaints, representing a shift from blaming to learning, encouraging police leaders to contribute to a culture where innovation and decision making without fear are supported.

> **CRITICAL THINKING ACTIVITY 9.2**
>
> **LEVEL 4**
>
> Compare the most common complaints about police officers with your views of the most challenging areas of investigation. Can you identify any themes?

DISCLOSURE

The Criminal Cases Review Commission's 2016 annual report claims the single most frequent cause of miscarriages of justice is a failure to disclose material that may have undermined the prosecution or assisted a defence. This implies that an examination of disclosure should feature in a chapter focused on measurements, enquiries and regulation.

Disclosure concerns pre-date the current legislation, and the cases of Stefan Kischko in 1975, Patricia Ward in 1993, and Michelle and Lisa Taylor in 1993 confirm the longevity of the issue.

In an adversarial justice system, the accumulation of material is the responsibility of the prosecution. The average suspect does not have the means or ability to conduct an investigation. Fairness is a tenet of English law, and the right to a fair trial is enshrined in the legislation of the Human Rights Act 1998. Yet these presumptions are being questioned in the current discussions of disclosure failings in criminal prosecutions, as illustrated in the 2017 case of *R v Allen* detailed in the policing spotlight section.

Disclosure in criminal proceedings is addressed in the Criminal Procedure and Investigations Act 1996 (CPIA) as amended by the Criminal Justice Act 2003. Investigators are obliged to record, retain and reveal relevant material. Material is defined as relevant if:

> ***It appears to the investigator, officer in charge or disclosure officer that it has some bearing on any offence under investigation or person being investigated, or on the surrounding circumstances of the case, unless it is incapable of having any impact on the case.***
>
> (CPIA 1996, Part II, s 23)

Evidence which the prosecution seeks to use in a trial will be notified to the defence in advance. The difficulties seem to arise in what is known as 'unused material'. Any material which may reasonably be objectively considered as capable of undermining a prosecution or assisting a defence, which is not relied on as evidence, should be disclosed to a defence. This is an organic decision which must be reviewed throughout an investigation and any subsequent trial. As investigations reveal new material or defences evolve, what may not have been relevant at an early stage may assume a new level of importance. Non-sensitive material should be disclosed without prejudice. Where a disclosure officer believes that material meets the relevance and disclosure test but believes to disclose it in its current form would create a serious prejudice to an important public interest, this material should be identified as 'sensitive' or 'highly sensitive', where disclosure would lead directly to loss of life or a threat to national security.

When sensitive or highly sensitive material meets the disclosure test, the options are to:

- disclose the material in a way that does not compromise the public interest in the issue;

- obtain a court order to withhold the material;

- abandon the prosecution;

- disclose the material where the overriding public interest is that of continuing the prosecution.

You are advised to seek further advice if you believe your disclosure includes sensitive material.

EVIDENCE-BASED POLICING

Paul Greenwood, author of the 'RAND study' of the 1970s (Greenwood et al, 1975), highlights that the investigative effort post charge has the largest chance of influencing the outcome of a prosecution, outlining a 20 per cent difference. This part of the investigative process is often viewed as administrative in nature and suffers from a lack of resourcing. The success or otherwise of an investigation is often judged by the success of a prosecution, as discussed in this chapter. To draw a study analogy, this is where your work is marked. To do justice to your investigation, you must ensure the case papers are professionally produced and contain all the material required to prove a case 'beyond all reasonable doubt'.

The 2017 report *Making it Fair* (HMICFRS, 2017) claims that 78 per cent of prosecution files are of poor quality, falling below acceptable standards. This is emphasised in routine casework, whereas complex cases are seen as generally good.

Richard Horwell QC in the Mouncher Investigation Report (2017) opined that:

> *Disclosure problems have blighted the criminal justice system for too long although disclosure guidelines manuals and policy are necessary. It is the mindset and experience of those who do disclosure that is paramount.*
>
> *Characteristically most recommendations focused on training or new ways of complying with various norms, rather than acknowledging the complexities of engaging or finding new ways to promote professional judgment or support reflective practice.*

The Criminal Procedure and Investigations Act was introduced with the aim of drawing together a plethora of policy, practice, common law, stated cases and legislation in one disclosure regime. Horwell suggests this must be complemented by an associated culture of openness, fairness and knowledge-based practice.

POLICING SPOTLIGHT

Liam Allen was charged with multiple counts of rape and sexual assault. The case hinged on the consent element of the events. As upsetting as such circumstances are, these are not unusual; sexual relationships mainly occur in private and as such investigations are challenging for all. What sets Allen apart is the trial's collapse. Text messages between the two parties revealed the existence of an existing relationship involving sexual activities and rape fantasies; further communication between the complainant and a friend confirmed no crimes had taken place. These had not been discovered in the investigation. The practicalities of analysing over 57,000 messages aside, paragraph 3.4 of the Criminal Procedure and Investigations Act 1996 (CPIA) code of practice highlights the requirement to:

> Pursue all reasonable lines of enquiry, whether these point towards or away from the suspect. What is reasonable in each case will depend on the particular circumstances. For example, where material is held on computer, it is a matter for the investigator to decide which material on the computer it is reasonable to enquire into, and in what manner.

Cases such as Allen (2017) highlight the practical challenges the digital era has introduced to investigators examining digital devices. The drive for fairness must be parallel to the proportionality aspect, which features in all decision making from the earliest stages to the culmination of all investigations. Is it reasonable to trawl through a victim's digital profile or should this only occur when a reason has been identified? A simple answer is not to look, in the words of the then Director of Public Prosecutions, Alison Saunders (2018), 'you cannot know, what you don't know'. Not turning the rock over to see what is underneath is not an option for any investigator, nor should it become an avenue of avoiding responsibility. In *R v Mills and Poole* [1998] 1 Cr App R 43, Lord Hutton outlines that the fruits of an investigation do not belong to the prosecution but are the property of the public to be used to ensure justice is done. Concentrate on the relevance of your investigation; when you identify a line of enquiry, pursue it until you are satisfied with the outcome. Your time is precious: make sure you spend it on relevant matters and not on general trawls in the hope of discovering something. Such is the capacity of devices in the digital age you will soon become overwhelmed.

CONCLUSION

Reviewing work and providing effective feedback is always challenging. Performing this in the context of a criminal investigation is even more so. Developing your professional practice is dependent upon recognising the history of oversight and evolution while adopting a paradigm that encourages its continuance. Reviews and enquiries must not trigger a defensive position. The only way to never make a mistake is never to make a decision: an undesirable trait in investigators. Providing you conduct your investigations in a proportionate, informed and professional manner, recording not only the what but also the why of your decision making while viewing a critical viewpoint as conducive to development, you have nothing to fear from accountability or oversight. Having examined investigation from both practitioner and academic viewpoints, we hope to have overcome the myths and conveyed the excitement and satisfaction investigating crime provides.

To quote a non-police officer, Nick Ross, *Crimewatch* presenter (1990), whose career involved working alongside detectives in the field of criminal investigation: *'Real detective work is not the stuff of Sherlock Holmes type intuition, but of persistence and a close relationship between the public and police'*. This observation from an independent observer of investigative practice brings us back to Chapter 1, an ideal point to finish this book.

SUMMARY OF KEY CONCEPTS

This chapter breaks down how your investigations are perceived and what occurs where investigations are found to be flawed. The content equips you to:

- evaluate measurements of investigative success;
- summarise formal enquiries and reports;
- explain how complaints are dealt with;
- assess your investigative material in accordance with disclosure guidelines.

CHECK YOUR KNOWLEDGE

1. Complete the blanks. CPIA advises that you should r___, r___ and r___ all relevant material.

2. Explain the progression of competence model.

3. Which organisation deals with the majority of complaints about police officers?

4. Which enquiry led to the reforming of an entire police force?

Sample answers to these questions are provided at the end of the book.

FURTHER READING

Brown, J (2020) *Police Complaints and Discipline*. House of Commons Briefing Paper. [online] Available at: https://researchbriefings.files.parliament.uk/documents/SN02056/SN02056.pdf (accessed 26 August 2021).
A briefing paper on contemporary practice surrounding complaints and discipline.

Hall, N, Grieve, J and Savage, S P (2009) *Policing and the Legacy of Lawrence*. Cullompton: Willan.
This text offers an in-depth examination of the impact of the Macpherson report on British policing.

SAMPLE ANSWERS

CHAPTER 1

CHECK YOUR KNOWLEDGE

1. SIO PIP3/4.

2. Burglary (Theft Act 1968, s 9).

3. • entered a building/part of a building;

   • as a trespasser;

   • dishonesty;

   • appropriation of property belonging to another;

   • intending to permanently deprive the other of it.

4. • high-profile policing;

   • detecting the offence;

   • media strategies;

   • communication skills;

   • crime prevention advice.

CHAPTER 2

CHECK YOUR KNOWLEDGE

1. d) when information is received.

2. Locard's

3. Section 19 of PACE

4.
- Information
- Intention
- Method
- Administration
- Risk assessment
- Communications
- Humanitarian issues

CHAPTER 3

CHECK YOUR KNOWLEDGE

1. Identify one source of information; when gaining information ask who else was present, creating a larger index of potential sources of information.

2.
- They were not involved.
- They have disposed of the stolen property.
- They have hiding places you do not know of.

3.
- People move from venue to venue.
- They may not be in the area again.
- Memories can be affected by passage of time or alcohol.
- People may have returned to different areas.

4.
- Forensic elimination is persuasive. However, suspect forensic awareness or a simple lack of forensic material may result in no forensic trace.
- Description. Successful descriptive ability and memory is dependent on a wide range of variables. Overall, people's descriptive ability is flawed.
- Alibi. Corroborate the account provided; establish the veracity.

CHAPTER 4

CRITICAL THINKING ACTIVITY 4.1

1. This relates to one of the core principles around obtaining first accounts and statements from witnesses.

2. John's initial account could be used to direct further examination of what he had seen or in some cases this could be introduced as the only evidence from John.

3. A public press release might assist in gathering further witnesses who may have been on the bus. You may also need to consult a supervisor about what other actions could be taken in the case.

4. John has been the victim of a crime and he has certain rights under the Victim Code, which are described later in this chapter.

CHECK YOUR KNOWLEDGE

1. You should obtain an account from a person who is intoxicated as this will be their first account; you should also obtain their details and assess their needs. You will need to inform them of their rights under the Victim Code (Ministry of Justice, 2020).

2. Section 16 is for witnesses who are vulnerable by virtue of a mental or physical condition, or are under 18, while section 17 is for witnesses who are afraid and have distress in testifying, so-called intimidated witnesses.

3. Determining that a witness is not credible too early undermines the overall integrity of the investigation and may lead to important evidence and details about the case being lost due to limited investigative activity taking place.

CHAPTER 5

CHECK YOUR KNOWLEDGE

1. Section 37 requires a person arrested by a constable to have been found by him/her at a place at or about the time the offence for which he/she was arrested is alleged to have been committed. This does not apply to these circumstances.

2. The significant statement should have been recorded and offered to the person to sign prior to the interview. You are advised to repeat the statement at the start of the interview after the caution, asking if they agree with the content or not. Questions about the content should be raised during the appropriate topic area.

3. Continue with your interview giving the interviewee the chance to answer all questions.

4. Tell

    Explain

    Describe

    Precisely

    In detail

    Exactly

CHAPTER 6

CHECK YOUR KNOWLEDGE

1.
    - stopping vehicles;
    - arresting suspects;
    - conducting stop searches;
    - using force;
    - conducting searches;
    - attending domestic abuse incidents.

2. Best evidence means the best available evidence; pursue the optimal evidence, leaving no doubt so as to achieve the criminal burden of proof.

3.
    - credibility;
    - qualified;
    - lack of bias.

4. • That no action is taken that should change data held on a digital device including a computer or mobile phone that may subsequently be relied upon as evidence in court.

   • Where a person finds it necessary to access original data held on a digital device that the person must be competent to do so and able to explain their actions and the implications of those actions on the digital evidence to a court.

   • That a trail or record of all actions taken that have been applied to the digital evidence should be created and preserved. An independent third-party forensic expert should be able to examine those processes and reach the same conclusion.

   • That the individual in charge of the investigation has overall responsibility to ensure that these principles are followed.

CHAPTER 7

CHECK YOUR KNOWLEDGE

1. This approach is practical 'good policing'. The question is whether it amounts to an immediate response. If so, then no authority is required; if there is an amount of planning, this suggests it is not and a surveillance authority would be required.

2. At this stage no relationship between the people exists and hence they are not a CHIS.

3. Juvenile CHIS are subject to a number of safeguards; in this situation, asking a juvenile to report on their parents' activities is not proportionate or appropriate.

4. No, you are monitoring conversations not communications.

CHAPTER 8

CHECK YOUR KNOWLEDGE

1. A critical incident can be defined as **any** incident where the effectiveness of the police response is **likely** to have a significant impact on the **confidence** of the victim, their family and/or the **community**.

2. Identify threats

3. Macpherson (1999)

4. Internal and external

CHAPTER 9

CHECK YOUR KNOWLEDGE

1. CPIA advises that you should **record, retain** and **reveal** all relevant material.

2. • Unconscious incompetence, where an organisation is unaware of failings.

    • Conscious incompetence, where awareness and steps to address this are formulated.

    • Conscious competence, where training, discussion and application surround the adoption of improved practices.

    • Unconscious competence, where practice is culturally embedded.

3. Police force Professional Standards Departments (PSD).

4. Patten report (1999)

REFERENCES

Adhami, E and Browne, D P (1996) *Major Crime Enquiries: Improving Expert Support for Detectives*. Special Interest Series Paper No. 9. London: Home Office.

Alison, L and Crego, J (eds) (2008) *Policing Critical Incidents*. Cullompton: Willan.

Association of Chief Police Officers (ACPO) (2005) *Practice Advice on Core Investigative Doctrine*. Wyboston: National Centre for Policing Excellence.

Association of Chief Police Officers (ACPO) (2006a) *Practice Advice on House to House Enquiries*. Wyboston: Centrex.

Association of Chief Police Officers (ACPO) (2006b) *Murder Investigation Manual*. Wyboston: National Centre for Policing Excellence.

Association of Chief Police Officers (ACPO) (2009) *Practice Advice on the Management of Priority and Volume Crime.* 2nd ed. Wyboston: National Police Improvement Agency.

Association of Chief Police Officers (ACPO) (2012a) *Practice Advice on Core Investigative Doctrine*. Wyboston: NPIA.

Association of Chief Police Officers (ACPO) (2012b) *Good Practice Guide for Digital Evidence*. [online] Available at: www.digital-detective.net/digital-forensics-documents/ACPO_Good_Practice_Guide_for_Digital_Evidence_v5.pdf (accessed 12 November 2021).

Baber, M (1999) *The Youth Justice and Criminal Evidence Bill (No. 99/40)*. London: House of Commons Library.

Baker, J T (1907) *The Art of Conversation: Twelve Golden Rules*. Evanston, IL: Correct English Publishing Company.

Baldwin, J (1993) Police Interview Techniques: Establishing Truth or Proof? *The British Journal of Criminology*, 33(3): 325–52.

Bichard, M (2004) *The Bichard Inquiry Report*. [online] Available at: https://dera.ioe.ac.uk/6394/1/report.pdf (accessed 17 November 2021).

Blair, T (1995) *Leader's Speech to Labour Party Conference*. Brighton. [online] Available at: www.britishpoliticalspeech.org/speech-archive.htm?speech=201 (accessed 12 November 2021).

British Security Industry Association (2020) Video Surveillance Systems. [online] Available at: www.bsia.co.uk (accessed 9 May 2021).

Brookman, F and Innes, M (2013) The Problem of Success: What Is a 'Good' Homicide Investigation? *Policing & Society*, 23(3).

Brown, J (2020) *Police Complaints and Discipline*. House of Commons Briefing Paper. [online] Available at: https://researchbriefings.files.parliament.uk/documents/SN02056/SN02056.pdf (accessed 26 August 2021).

Brown, R and Smith, R G (2018) Exploring the Relationship between Organised Crime and Volume Crime. *Trends and Issues in Crime and Criminal Justice* No 565. [online] Available at: https://apo.org.au/sites/default/files/resource-files/2018-12/apo-nid209716.pdf (accessed 12 November 2021).

Bryant, R P (2009) Forms of Reasoning and the Analysis of Intelligence in Criminal Investigation. In Tong, S, Bryant, R and Horvath, M (eds) *Understanding Criminal Investigation*. Chichester: Wiley.

Burgess, R G (1984) *In the Field: An Introduction to Field Research*. London: Allen & Unwin.

Burton, M, Evans, R and Sanders, A (2006) *An Evaluation of the Use of Special Measures for Vulnerable and Intimidated Witnesses*. London: Home Office; Research, Development and Statistics Directorate.

Byford, L (1981) *The Yorkshire Ripper Case. Review of the Police Investigation of the Case*. [online] Available at: https://assets.publishing.service.gov.uk/government/uploads/system/uploads/attachment_data/file/100353/1941-Byford_part_1_.pdf (accessed 12 November 2021).

Caddy, B, Taylor, G R and Linacre, A M T (2008) *A Review of the Science of Low Template DNA Analysis*. London: Home Office.

Canter, D (2010) *Forensic Psychology: A Very Short Introduction*. Oxford: Oxford University Press.

Charles, C (2012) *Special Measures for Vulnerable and Intimidated Witnesses: Research Exploring the Decisions and Actions Taken by Prosecutors in a Sample of CPS Case Files*. London: Crown Prosecution Service.

Chevroulet, C, Paterson, H M, Yu, A, Chew, E and Kemp, R I (2021) The Impact of Recall Timing on the Preservation of Eyewitness Memory. *Psychiatry, Psychology and Law*, 1–16.

Cohen, S (2002) *Folk Devils and Moral Panics*. 30th anniversary ed. London: Routledge.

Cole, G A (2004) *Management Theory and Practice*. 6th ed. London: Thomson.

College of Policing (2013a) *Investigative Interviewing.* [online] Available at: www.app.college.police.uk/app-content/investigations/investigative-interviewing (accessed 12 November 2021).

College of Policing (2013b) *Authorised Professional Practice: National Decision Model.* [online] Available at: www.app.college.police.uk/app-content/national-decision-model (accessed 12 November 2021).

College of Policing (2016) Guidance on Police Media Relations. [online] Available at: www.app.college.police.uk/app-content/engagement-and-communication/media-relations (accessed 12 November 2021).

College of Policing (2020a) *Authorised Professional Practice: Briefing and De-briefing.* [online] Available at: www.app.college.police.uk/app-content/operations/briefing-and-debriefing (accessed 15 August 2021).

College of Policing (2020b) *Obtaining Initial Accounts from Victims and Witnesses: Guidelines for First Responders.* [online] Available at: https://assets.college.police.uk/s3fs-public/2020-11/Initial_Accounts_Guidelines.pdf (accessed 21 November 2021).

College of Policing (2021a) *Authorised Professional Practice: Media Relations.* [online] Available at: www.app.college.police.uk/app-content/engagement-and-communication/media-relations (accessed 10 August 2021).

College of Policing (2021b) *Authorised Professional Practice: Communications Strategy.* [online] Available at: www.app.college.police.uk/app-content/investigations/investigative-strategies/communications-strategy (accessed 30 August 2021).

College of Policing (2021c) *Authorised Professional Practice: Critical Incident Management.* [online] Available at: www.app.college.police.uk/app-content/critical-incident-management/types-of-critical-incident/#principles (accessed 27 August 2021).

Collins, K, Harker, N and Antonopoulos, G A (2017) The Impact of the Registered Intermediary on Adults' Perceptions of Child Witnesses: Evidence from a Mock Cross Examination. *European Journal on Criminal Policy and Research*, 23(2): 211–25.

Commissioner of Police of the Metropolis (Appellant) v DSD and another (Respondents) [2018] UKSC 11 on appeal from [2015] EWCA Civ 646.

Conan Doyle, A (1892) *The Adventure of Silver Blaze*. London: George Newnes.

Cook, T and Tattersall, A (2010) *Blackstone's Senior Investigating Officers' Handbook*. Oxford: Oxford University Press.

Cooren, F (2000) *Organizing Property of Communication*. Philadelphia, PA: John Benjamins Publishing Company.

Crandon, G L and Dunne, S (1997) Symbiosis or Vassalage? The Media and the Law Enforcers – the Case of Avon and Somerset Police. *Policing & Society*, 8(1): 77–91.

Crimewatch File. The Red Connection (1990) British Broadcasting Corporation. 15 August 1990.

Criminal Cases Review Commission (2016) *Annual Report 2015/2016*. [online] Available at: https://s3-eu-west-2.amazonaws.com/jotwpublic-prod-storage-1cxo1dnrmkg14/uploads/sites/5/2021/04/CCRC-Annual-Report-and-Accounts-2015-16-HC244-Web-Accessible-v0.2-2.pdf (accessed 17 November 2021).

Criminal Justice Joint Inspectorate (2009) Report of a Joint Thematic Review of Victim and Witness Experiences in the Criminal Justice System (No 1). London: CJJI.

Crown Prosecution Service (CPS) (2014) *Victims' Right to Review Guidance* (No 1). London: CPS.

Crown Prosecution Service (CPS) (2018) *The Code for Crown Prosecutors*. London: CPS.

Crown Prosecution Service (CPS) (2019a) Cybercrime Prosecution Guidance. [online] Available at: www.cps.gov.uk/legal-guidance/cybercrime-prosecution-guidance (accessed 12 November 2021).

Crown Prosecution Service (CPS) (2019b) Expert Evidence. [online] Available at: www.cps.gov.uk/legal-guidance/expert-evidence (accessed 12 November 2021).

Dando, C J and Ormerod, T C (2017) Analyzing Decision Logs to Understand Decision Making in Serious Crime Investigations. *Human Factors: The Journal of the Human Factors and Ergonomics Society*, 59(8): 1188–203.

Denyer, J R (2011) Video Recorded Evidence – (2011) 175 JPN 253. *Criminal Law and Justice Weekly (Formerly Justice of the Peace)*.

Dewey, J (1910) *How We Think*. Boston, MA: DC Heath.

Ditton, J and Duffy, J (1983) Bias in the Newspaper Reporting of Crime News. *British Journal of Criminology*, 23(2): 159–65.

DiYanni, R (2016) *Critical and Creative Thinking: A Brief Guide for Teachers*. Chichester: Wiley Blackwell.

Doak, J and McGourlay, C (2009) *Criminal Evidence in Context*. London: Routledge Cavendish.

Doak, J and McGourlay, C (2012) *Evidence in Context*. 3rd ed. Abingdon: Routledge.

DPP v Morrison [2003] EWHC 683.

Durston, G (2011) *Evidence: Text & Materials*. Oxford: Oxford University Press.

Eck, J E (1979) *Managing Crime Assignments – The Burglary Investigation Decision Model Replication*. Washington, DC: Police Executive Research Forum.

Eck, J E and Rossmo, D K (2019) The New Detective. *Criminology & Public Policy*, 18(3): 601–22.

Ellison, L (1999) The Protection of Vulnerable Witnesses in Court: An Anglo-Dutch Comparison. *The International Journal of Evidence & Proof*, 3(1): 29–43.

Ellison, M (2014) *The Stephen Lawrence Independent Review: Possible Corruption and the Role of Undercover Policing in the Stephen Lawrence Case*. Vol. 1. London: Home Office.

Ewin, R (2015) The Vulnerable and Intimidated Witness: A Socio-legal Analysis of Special Measures. *Journal of Applied Psychology and Social Science*, 1(2): 31–54.

Ewin, R (2016) The Vulnerable and Intimidated Witness: A Study of the Special Measure Practitioner. *Journal of Applied Psychology and Social Science*, 2(1): 12–40.

Feist, A (1999) *The Effective Use of the Media in Serious Crime Investigations*. London: Home Office.

Ferraro, K (1995) *Fear of Crime: Interpreting Victimization Risk*. New York: State University of New York, Albany.

Fleming, J and Rhodes, R A W (2005) Bureaucracy, Contracts and Networks: The Unholy Trinity and the Police. *Australian & New Zealand Journal of Criminology*, 38(2): 192–205.

Foot, P (1967) The Problem of Abortion and the Doctrine of the Double Effect. *Oxford Review*, 5: 5–15.

Galton, F (1892) *Finger Prints*. London. Macmillan. [online] Available at: https://galton.org/books/finger-prints/galton-1892-fingerprints-1up.pdf (accessed 12 November 2021).

Ghani v Jones [1970] 1 QB 693.

Gill, P (1987) Clearing up Crime: The Big 'Con'. *Journal of Law and Society*, 14(2): 254–65.

Gillespie, M and McLaughlin, E (2002) Media and the Shaping of Public Attitudes. *Criminal Justice Matters*, 49(Autumn): 8–9 & 23.

Greenwood, P W, Chaiken, J M, Petersilia, J and Prusoff, L (1975) *The Criminal Investigation Process Volumes 1–3*. Santa Monica, CA. Rand Corporation.

Griffiths, B (2009) Doing the Right Thing: A Personal and Organisational Journey of Change in Homicide Investigation in the Metropolitan Police Service. In Hall, N, Grieve, J and Savage, S P (eds) *Policing and the Legacy of Lawrence*. Cullompton: Willan.

Grinshteyn, E G (2013) *Causes and Consequences of Fear of Crime: The Impact of Fear of Crime on Behavioral Health Outcomes and Behavioral Health Treatment*. [online] Available at: www.academia.edu/47054159/Causes_and_Consequences_of_Fear_of_Crime_The_Impact_of_Fear_of_Crime_on_Behavioral_Health_Outcomes_and_Behavioral_Health_Treatment (accessed 12 November 2021).

Haber, L and Haber, R N (1998) Criteria for Judging the Admissibility of Eyewitness Testimony of Long Past Events. *Psychology, Public Policy, and Law*, 4(4): 1135–59.

Hall, S, Evans, J and Nixon, S (eds) (2013) *Representation: Cultural Representation and Signifying Practices*. 2nd ed. London: Sage.

Hancock, V (2004) Criminal Justice, Public Opinion, Fear and Popular Politics. In Muncie, J and Wilson, D (eds) *Student Handbook of Criminal Justice and Criminology*. London: Cavendish.

Henderson, E (2015) Theoretically Speaking: English Judges and Advocates Discuss the Changing Theory of Cross-examination. *Criminal Law Review*, 12: 929.

Her Majesty's Inspectorate of Constabulary and Fire & Rescue Services (HMICFRS) (2001) *Winning the Race: Embracing Diversity*. [online] Available at: www.justiceinspectorates.gov.uk/hmicfrs/media/winning-the-race-embracing-diversity-20010114.pdf (accessed 17 November 2021).

Her Majesty's Inspectorate of Constabulary and Fire & Rescue Services (HMICFRS) (2014) *Crime Recording: Making the Victim Count*. [online] Available at: www.justiceinspectorates.gov.uk/hmicfrs/wp-content/uploads/crime-recording-making-the-victim-count.pdf (accessed 17 November 2021).

Her Majesty's Inspectorate of Constabulary and Fire & Rescue Services (HMICFRS) (2017) *Making it Fair. A Joint Inspection of the Disclosure of Unused Material in Volume Crown Court Cases.* [online] Available at: www.justiceinspectorates.gov.uk/cjji/inspections/making-it-fair-the-disclosure-of-unused-material-in-volume-crown-court-cases (accessed 23 August 2021).

Her Majesty's Inspectorate of Constabulary and Fire & Rescue Services (HMICFRS) (2018) *Public Perceptions of Policing in England and Wales 2018.* [online] Available at: www.justiceinspectorates.gov.uk/hmicfrs/publications/public-perceptions-of-policing-in-england-and-wales-2018/#crime (accessed 27 August 2021).

Her Majesty's Inspectorate of Constabulary and Fire & Rescue Services (HMICFRS) (2020) *Crime Data Integrity Programme (Crime Recording Inspections)*. [online] Available at www.justiceinspectorates.gov.uk/hmicfrs/our-work/article/crime-data-integrity (accessed 12 November 2021).

Hicks, S J and Sales, B D (2006) *Criminal Profiling: Developing an Effective Science and Practice*. Washington, DC: American Psychological Association.

Hill v CC West Yorkshire Police [1989].

Home Office (1992) *Investigative Interviewing*. Police Circular 22/92. London: Home Office.

Home Office (2000) *Achieving Best Evidence in Criminal Proceedings: Guidance for Vulnerable or Intimidated Witnesses, Including children. Implementing the Speaking up for Justice Report*. Consultation paper. London: Home Office.

Home Office (2015) *Acquisition and Disclosure of Communications Data: Code of Practice.* [online] Available at: https://assets.publishing.service.gov.uk/government/uploads/system/uploads/attachment_data/file/426248/Acquisition_and_Disclosure_of_Communications_Data_Code_of_Practice_March_2015.pdf (accessed 17 August 2021).

Home Office (2018a) *Safeguarding Body Worn Video Data.* London: Home Office.

Home Office (2018b) *Covert Human Intelligence Sources: Revised Code of Practice.* [online] Available at: https://assets.publishing.service.gov.uk/government/uploads/system/uploads/attachment_data/file/742042/20180802_CHIS_code_.pdf (accessed 12 November 2021).

Home Office (2020) *Operational Briefings and Planning.* London: Home Office.

Home Office (2021) *Crime Recording General Rules.* [online] Available at: https://assets.publishing.service.gov.uk/government/uploads/system/uploads/attachment_data/file/992833/count-general-jun-2021.pdf (accessed 12 November 2021).

Horwell, R (2017) *Mouncher Investigation Report.* [online] Available at: https://assets.publishing.service.gov.uk/government/uploads/system/uploads/attachment_data/file/629725/mouncher_report_web_accessible_july_2017.pdf (accessed 12 November 2021).

Hoyle, C and Zedner, L (2007) Victims, Victimization and Criminal Justice. *The Oxford Handbook of Criminology,* 4.

Hunter, J and Cox, M (2005) *Forensic Archaeology: Advances in Theory and Practice.* London: Routledge.

Independent Office for Police Conduct (IOPC) (2019) *Police Complaints Statistics for England and Wales 2018/19.* London. IOPC.

Independent Office for Police Conduct (IOPC) (2020) *IOPC Learning Strategy: Improving Policing by Identifying and Sharing Learning from Our Work.* London: IOPC.

Independent Police Complaints Commission (2009) *IPCC Report into the Contact between Fiona Pilkington and Leicestershire Constabulary 2004–2007.* [online] Available at: www.report-it.org.uk/files/ipcc_report-fiona-pilkington-leicestershire.pdf (accessed 17 November 2021).

Innes, M (1999) The Media as an Investigative Resource in Murder Enquiries. *British Journal of Criminology,* 39(2): 269–86.

Innes, M (2002) The 'Process Structures' of Police Homicide Investigations. *British Journal of Criminology*, 42(4): 669–88.

Innes, M (2003) *Investigating Murder: Detective Work and the Police Response to Criminal Homicide*. Oxford: Oxford University Press.

Innes, M (2006) Policing Uncertainty: Countering Terror through Community Intelligence and Democratic Policing. *The Annals of the American Academy of Political and Social Science*, 605(1): 222–41.

Innes, M (2007) Investigation, Order and Major Crime Enquiries. In Newburn, T, Williamson, T and Wright, A (eds) *Handbook of Criminal Investigation*. Cullompton: Willan.

Innes, M (2010) Criminal Legacies: Community Impact Assessments and Defining 'Success' and 'Harm' in Police Homicide Investigations. *Journal of Contemporary Criminal Justice*, 26(4): 367–81.

Ipsos (2015) *Views on PEEL Assessments*. [online] Available at: www.ipsos.com/sites/default/files/publication/1970-01/sri-crime-views-of-peel-assessments-2015.pdf (accessed 12 November 2021).

Irving, B and Dunninghan, C (1993) *Human Factors in the Quality Control of CID Investigations*. Research no 201. Criminal Justice UK.

Ivey v Genting Casinos [2017] UKSC 67.

Javid, S (2018) in *Serious Organised Crime Strategy*. [online] Available at: https://assets.publishing.service.gov.uk/government/uploads/system/uploads/attachment_data/file/752850/SOC-2018-web.pdf (accessed 12 November 2021).

Jay, A (2014) *Independent Inquiry into Child Sexual Exploitation in Rotherham*. [online] Available at: www.rotherham.gov.uk/downloads/file/279/independent-inquiry-into-child-sexual-exploitation-in-rotherham (accessed 12 November 2021).

Kerslake, B (2018) *An Independent Review into the Preparedness for, and Emergency Response to, the Manchester Arena Attack on 22nd May 2017*. [online] Available at: www.jesip.org.uk/uploads/media/Documents%20Products/Kerslake_Report_Manchester_Are.pdf (accessed 31 August 2021).

Klockars, C B (1985) The Dirty Harry Problem. In Elliston, F A and Feldberg, M (eds) *Moral Issues in Police Work*. Totowa, NJ: Rowman and Allenheld.

Lawrence, D (2009) Foreword. In Hall, N, Grieve, J and Savage, S P (eds) *Policing and the Legacy of Lawrence*. Cullompton: Willan.

Lea, S J and Lynn, N (2012) Dialogic Reverberations: Police, Domestic Abuse, and the Discontinuance of Cases. *Journal of Interpersonal Violence*, 27(15): 3091–114.

Lefkowitz, J (2010) Psychological Attributes of Policemen: A Review of Research and Opinion. *Journal of Social Sciences*, 31(1): 3–26.

Leveson, B (2012) *An Inquiry into the Culture, Practices and Ethics of the Press*. [online] Available at: www.gov.uk/government/publications/leveson-inquiry-report-into-the-culture-practices-and-ethics-of-the-press (accessed 12 November 2021).

Lister, S, Burn, D and Pina-Sanchez, J (2018) *Exploring the Impacts of Police Use of Body Worn Video Cameras at Incidents of Domestic Abuse*. N8 Policing Research Partnership. [online] Available at: https://n8prp.org.uk/wp-content/uploads/2018/09/Body-Worn-Video.pdf (accessed 17 August 2021).

Locard, E (1923) *Manuel de technique policière (enquête criminelle)*. Paris: Payot.

Loftus, E F and Palmer, J C (1974) Reconstruction of Automobile Destruction: An Example of the Interaction between Language and Memory. *Journal of Verbal Learning and Verbal Behaviour*, 13(5): 585–9.

Macpherson, C (2001) The Youth Justice and Criminal Evidence Act 1999: Achieving Best Evidence? *Medicine, Science and the Law*, 41(3): 230–6.

Macpherson, W (1999) *The Stephen Lawrence Inquiry: Report of an Inquiry by Sir William Macpherson of Cluny*. London. HMSO.

Malone v The United Kingdom: ECHR 2 August 1984.

Maras, K, Dando, C, Stephenson, H, Lambrechts, A, Anns, S and Gaigg, S (2020) The Witness-Aimed First Account (WAFA): A New Technique for Interviewing Autistic Witnesses and Victims. *Autism*, 24(6): 1449–67.

Marsh, I and Melville, G (2014) *Crime, Justice and the Media*. 2nd ed. Oxford: Routledge.

Mawby, R C (1999) Visibility, Transparency and Police-media Relations. *Policing and Society*, 9(3): 263–86.

McDermott, Y (2013) The Admissibility and Weight of Written Witness Testimony in International Criminal Law: A Socio-legal Analysis. *Leiden Journal of International Law*, 26(4): 971–89.

Metropolitan Police (2017) *Crime Assessment Policy*. London: Metropolitan Police.

Mills and Poole, R v United Kingdom (1998) HCR App R 43.

Ministry of Justice (MoJ) (2011) *Achieving Best Evidence in Criminal Proceedings: Guidance on Interviewing Victims and Witnesses, and Guidance on Using Special Measures*. 1st ed. London: Ministry of Justice.

Ministry of Justice (MoJ) (2015) *Criminal Procedure and Investigations Act, Code of Practice*. [online] Available at: www.gov.uk/government/publications/criminal-procedure-and-investigations-act-code-of-practice (accessed 16 August 2021).

Ministry of Justice (MoJ) (2020) *The Code of Practice for Victims of Crime in England and Wales*. [online] Available at: www.gov.uk/government/publications/the-code-of-practice-for-victims-of-crime (accessed 12 November 2021).

Myhill, A and Bradford, B (2012) Can Police Enhance Public Confidence by Improving Quality of Services? Results from Two surveys in England and Wales. *Policing and Society*, 22(4): 397–425.

National Police Chiefs Council (NPCC) (2015) *An SIO's Guide to Investigating Unexpected Death and Serious Harm in Healthcare Settings*. [online] Available at: https://library.college.police.uk/docs/NPCC/2015-SIO-Guide-Investigating-Deaths-and-Serious-Harm-in-Healthcare-Settings-v10-6.pdf (accessed 12 November 2021).

National Police Improvement Agency (NPIA) (2009) *Practice Advice on the Management of Priority and Volume Crime*. [online] Available at: https://library.college.police.uk/docs/acpo/VCMM-191109.pdf (accessed 12 November 2021).

Newburn, T, Williamson, T and Wright, A (2007) *Handbook of Criminal Investigation*. Cullompton: Willan.

Neyroud, P and Beckley, A (2001) *Policing, Ethics and Human Rights*. Cullompton: Willan.

Nield, R, Milne, R, Bull, R and Marlow, K (2003) The Youth Justice and Criminal Evidence Act 1999 and the Interviewing of Vulnerable Groups: A Practitioner's Perspective. *Legal and Criminological Psychology*, 8(2): 223–8.

O'Mahony, B (2013) *How Do Intermediaries Experience Their Role in Facilitating Communication for Vulnerable Defendants?* Doctoral dissertation, University of Portsmouth.

O'Mahony, B M, Creaton, J, Smith, K and Milne, R (2016) Developing a Professional Identity in a New Work Environment: The Views of Defendant Intermediaries Working in the Criminal Courts. *Journal of Forensic Practice*, 18(2): 155–66.

O'Mahony, B M, Smith, K and Milne, B (2011) The Early Identification of Vulnerable Witnesses Prior to an Investigative Interview. *The British Journal of Forensic Practice*, 13(2): 114–23.

O'Neal, E N (2019) 'Victim is Not Credible': The Influence of Rape Culture on Police Perceptions of Sexual Assault Complainants. *Justice Quarterly*, 36(1): 127–60.

O'Neill, M (2018) *Key Challenges in Criminal Investigation*. Bristol: Policy Press.

Office for National Statistics (2016) Crime in England and Wales: Year Ending March 2016. [online] Available at www.ons.gov.uk/releases/crimeinenglandandwalesyearending mar2016 (accessed 17 November 2021).

Office for National Statistics (2020) Crime in England and Wales: Year Ending December 2020. [online] Available at: www.ons.gov.uk/peoplepopulationandcommunity/ crimeandjustice/bulletins/crimeinenglandandwales/yearendingdecember2020 (accessed 12 November 2021).

Omychund v Barker 1744 125 ER.

Onassis v Vergottis [1968] 2 Lloyds Rep 403.

Owens, C, Mann, D and McKenna, R (2014) *The Essex Body Worn Video Trial: The Impact of Body Worn Video on Criminal Justice Outcomes of Domestic Abuse Incidents*. [online] Available at: https://bja.ojp.gov/sites/g/files/xyckuh186/files/bwc/pdfs/bwv_reportesstrial.pdf (accessed 12 November 2021).

Oxburgh, G, Ost, J and Cherryman, J (2012) Police Interviews with Suspected Child Sex Offenders: Does Use of Empathy and Question Type Influence the Amount of Investigation Relevant Information Obtained? *Psychology, Crime & Law*, 18(3): 259–73.

Oxburgh, L, Gabbert, F, Milne, R and Cherryman, J (2016) Police Officers' Perceptions and Experiences with Mentally Disordered Suspects. *International Journal of Law and Psychiatry*, 49: 138–46.

Parliamentary Office of Science and Technology (2001) *Biometrics and Security*, No 165. London: Parliament.

Patten, C (1999) *A New Beginning: Policing in Northern Ireland. The Report of the Independent Commission for Policing in Northern Ireland.* [online] Available at: https://cain.ulster.ac.uk/issues/police/patten/patten99.pdf (accessed 17 November 2021).

Peel, R (1829) *Principles of Law Enforcement.* [online] Available at: www.gov.uk/government/publications/policing-by-consent (accessed 21 December 2021).

Pigot, T (1989) *Report of the Advisory Group on Video-recorded Evidence.* London: Home Office.

Plotnikoff, J and Woolfson, R (2007) *The 'Go-between': Evaluation of Intermediary Pathfinder Projects.* Research Summary, 1. London: NSPCC/The Nuffield Foundation.

Police and Criminal Evidence Act 1984. [online] Available at: www.legislation.gov.uk/ukpga/1984/60/contents (accessed 12 November 2021).

Police.UK (2021) Automatic Number Plate Recognition. [online] Available at: www.police.uk/advice/advice-and-information/rs/road-safety/automatic-number-plate-recognition-anpr (accessed 14 May 2021).

R v Barker and *R v T* [1998] 2 NZLR 257 (CA).

R (Bridges) v Chief Constable of South Wales Police and Ors [2020]. EWCA 1058.

R v Camberwell Green Youth Court [2005] UKHL 4.

R v Dudley and Stephens (1884) 14 QBD 273.

R v E [2018] EWCA 2426 (Crim).

R v Hodges [2003] EWCA Crim 290.

R v Hoey [2007] NICC 49.

R v Johnson [2005] EWCA Crim 971.

R v JP [2014] EWCA Crim 2064.

R v Makanjuola [1995] 3 All ER 730 (CA).

R v Salisbury [2005] EWCA Crim 3107.

R v Turnbull and Camelo (1977) Q.B.224

Rand Corporation (1975) *The Criminal Investigation Process* (Vols 1–3). Santa Monica, CA: Rand Corporation.

Regulation of Investigatory Powers Act 2000. [online] Available at: www.legislation.gov.uk/ukpga/2000/23/contents (accessed 12 November 2021).

Reith, C (1956) *A New Study of Police History*. Edinburgh: Oliver and Boyd.

Ridley, A, Van Rheede, V and Wilcock, R (2015) Interviews, Intermediaries and Interventions: Mock-jurors', Police Officers' and Barristers' Perceptions of a Child Witness Interview. *Investigative Interviewing: Research and Practice*, 7(1): 21–35.

Roberts, P (2007) Law and Criminal Investigation. In Newburn, T, Williamson, T and Wright, A (eds) *Handbook of Criminal Investigation*. Cullompton: Willan.

Roberts, P and Zuckerman, A A S (2010) *Criminal Evidence*. 2nd ed. Oxford: Oxford University Press.

Rousseau, J-J and Cranston, M (2005) *The Social Contract*. London: Penguin.

Royal Commission on Criminal Justice (1981) *Report of the Royal Commission on Criminal Justice*. [online] Available at: www.gov.uk/government/publications/report-of-the-royal-commission-on-criminal-justice (accessed 17 November 2021).

Saunders, A (2018) Disclosure – Joint Statement from Director of Public Prosecutions and Chair of National Police Chiefs' Council. [online] Available at: www.cps.gov.uk/cps/news/disclosure-joint-statement-alison-saunders-director-public-prosecutions-and-sara-thornton (accessed 12 November 2021).

Scarman, L S (1981) *The Brixton Disorders 10–12 April 1981: Report of an Enquiry*. London: HMSO.

Schank, R C (1977) Rules and Topics in Conversation. *Cognitive Science*, 1(4): 421–41.

Schedule 2, The Police (Conduct) Regulations 2020. [online] Available at: www.legislation.gov.uk/uksi/2020/4/schedule/2/made (accessed 17 November 2021).

Shepherd, E and Griffiths, A (2013) *Investigative Interviewing: The Conversation Management Approach*. 2nd ed. Oxford: Oxford University Press.

Shepherd, J (2015) *Making Sense of Crime*. [online] Available at: https://senseaboutscience.org/wp-content/uploads/2016/11/Makingsenseofcrime.pdf (accessed 12 November 2021).

Simon, H A (1956) Rational Choice and the Structure of the Environment. *Psychological Review*, 63(2): 129–38.

Simon, H A (1990) Invariants of Human Behaviour. *Annual Review of Psychology*, 637(41): 1–20.

Sir Cliff Richard v BBC and Chief Constable of South Yorkshire Police [2018] EWHC 1837.

Smith, J (1993) *Misogynies*. London: Faber & Faber.

Smith, J (2003) *The Shipman Inquiry, Second Report: The Police Investigation of March 1998*. [online] Available at: https://assets.publishing.service.gov.uk/government/uploads/system/uploads/attachment_data/file/273226/5853.pdf (accessed 12 November 2021).

Sprack, J (2011) *A Practical Approach to Criminal Procedure*. Oxford: Oxford University Press.

Starmer, K (1999) *European Human Rights Law: The Human Rights Act 1998 and the European Convention on Human Rights*. London: Legal Action Group.

Stelfox, P (2012) *Criminal Investigation: An Introduction to Principles and Practice*. London: Routledge.

Strathern, M (1997) 'Improving Ratings': Audit in the British University System. *European Review (Chichester, England)*, 5(3): 305–21.

The Sun (2015) 1 in 5 British Muslims have Sympathy for ISIS. 23 November 2015, p 1.

Swinney v Chief Constable of Northumbria Police Force [1997] QB 464 Court of Appeal.

Thomas, R (2004) *Surveillance: Citizens and the State-Constitution Committee Report*. [online] Available at: https://publications.parliament.uk/pa/ld200809/ldselect/ldconst/18/1803.htm (accessed 12 November 2021).

Tomlinson, M (2000) Frustrating Patten: Commentary on the Patten Report – A New Beginning: Policing in Northern Ireland. The Report of the Independent Commission on Policing for Northern Ireland. *Irish Journal of Sociology (IJS)*, 10(1): 103–9.

Tong, S, Bryant, R and Horvath, M (2009) *Understanding Criminal Investigation*. Malden, MA: Wiley.

Topping, J R (2008) Community Policing in Northern Ireland: A Resistance Narrative. *Policing and Society*, 18(4): 377–96.

Tversky, A and Kahneman, D (1974) Judgment under Uncertainty: Heuristics and Biases. *Science*, 185(4157): 1124–31.

Tyler, T R (2005) Viewing *CSI* and the Threshold of Guilt: Managing Truth and Justice in Reality and Fiction. *Yale Law Journal*, 115: 1050–85.

Waldron, J (2003) Security and Liberty: The Image of Balance. *Journal of Political Philosophy*, 11(2): 191–210.

Walsh, D W and Milne, R (2008) Keeping the PEACE? A Study of Investigative Interviewing Practices in the Public Sector. *Legal and Criminological Psychology*, 13: 39–57.

Ward, A (2020) Merseyside Use of Body Worn Video a Success. [online] Available at: www.college.police.uk/article/merseyside-use-body-worn-video-success (accessed 12 November 2021).

Wattis, L (2018) *Revisiting the Yorkshire Ripper Murders: Histories of Gender, Violence and Victimhood*. Cham: Springer International Publishing.

Williamson, T (2007) Psychology and Criminal Investigation. In Newburn, T, Williamson, T and Wright, A (eds) *Handbook of Criminal Investigation*. Cullompton: Willan.

Wilson, J Q and Kelling, G L (1982) Broken Windows: The Police and Neighborhood Safety. *Atlantic Monthly*, 211: 29–38.

Wilson, W (2008) *Criminal Law: Doctrine and Theory*. Harlow: Pearson Education.

Wright, M, Cook, T, Pinder, D, Gregory, A and Shaw, G (2015) T.I.E. Practice, Terminology, Tactics and Training. *The Journal of Homicide and Major Incident Investigation*, 10(2).

INDEX

5WH approach, 23, 48, 99

ABC model, 47, 51
academia see higher education, partnerships
Account, Clarification and Challenge, 19
accountability, 46, 175
Achieving Best Evidence (ABE), 70
action decisions, 42
activities
  assessing success, 167
  bias and witness credibility, 122
  complaints, 177
  crime scenes, 109
  critical incidents, 150
  evaluating the golden hour principles, 34
  H2H enquiries, 52
  legislation and practice, 9
  media strategies, 55
  necessity, 134
  presentations and briefings, 155
  privacy, 139
  rapport in interviews, 103
  special measures, 72
  specialties in policing, 3
  spotlight on theft allegation, 6
  spotlight on victims, 10
  vulnerable witnesses, 68
Adhami, E, 156
ADVOKATE mnemonic, 7
age, of witnesses, 71
Alison, L, 147
analysis, 174

appropriate adults, 73
arrest strategies, 32
art, of criminal investigation, 2, 14
authorisation levels
  declaration of critical incidents, 150
  for covert methods, 141, 153
autistic people, equal memory skills of, 66
automatic number plate recognition (ANPR), 114, 128

bad character evidence, 96–8
Baker, J T, 98
Beckley, A, 128, 133, 168
behavioural investigative advisors (BIAs), 117
bias, in investigation process, 8, 21, 42, 46, 48, 174
Bichard Report, the, 165, 172
Birmingham Six enquiry, the (1991), 3, 8, 84
Blair, Tony, 36
Blunkett, David, 96
body-worn video (BWV), 115
Bradford, B, 28
briefings, 154, see also IIMARCH briefing model
Brixton riots, the, 3, 8, 169
Brookman, F, 166
Brown, R, 25
Browne, D P, 156
Bryant, R P, 99
Burn, D, 117
Byford Report, the, 58, 165, 169

Canter, D, 118, 119
Cardiff Three, the (1988), 84
case studies
  car theft in tourist areas, 46
  collapse of sexual assault case, 179
  crime scene mismanagement, 30
  critical incidents, 152
  drawing on experts, 120
  first witness accounts, 66
  Harold Shipman, 22
  influence of Human Rights Act, 132
  information passed to offenders, 33
  necessity and the Mignonette, 134
  profiling, 118
  victim support and special measures, 69, 72
  vulnerable witness, 67–8
  Whitehaven shootings, 35
  witness credibility, 76
  Yorkshire Ripper, 58
caution, use of, 91, 92
CCTV (closed-circuit television), 19, 25, 28, 56, 67, 103, 113, 114, 115, 138, 153
CD. see Practice Advice on Core Investigative Doctrine (CD)
challenges, in interviews, 102
change, as result of poor practice, 168

INDEX

Child Sex Offenders Disclosure Scheme, 96
CIAPOAR mnemonic, 44
citizen journalism, 158
Civil Contingencies Act (2004), 120
CLAD mnemonic, 29
Cohen, S, 148
Cole, G A, 85
collateral intrusion, 137
College of Policing, 33, 44, 50, 53, 147, 148
communications data, 111
communications strategy, 152–9
communities, engaging with, 28, 50, 51, 113
community impact assessments (CIAs), 150–1
compensation, 78
competence
  competence model, 171
  legal presumption of, 74
complaints process, 79, 175
complex cases
  definitions of, 146
Confait, Maxwell, 169
contamination, of evidence, 27, 31–2, 65, 158
Contempt of Court Act (1981), 157
convictions
  as measure of success, 166
  previous, 96
Cooren, F, 156
cordons, used at crime scene, 25, 27
Core Investigative Doctrine, 18, 44, 54, 55, 77
corruption probes, 3

counter-terrorism, 2
court, assistance in, 69, 74
covert methods
  covert human intelligence sources (CHISs), 31, 128, 131, 135, 139–41
  public view of, 128
craft, of criminal investigation, 2, 5, 14
Crandon, G L, 157
Cranston, M, 128
credibility, of witnesses, 75–6, 121
crime
  crime scenes, 24
  impact of, 2
  perceptions of, 11–13
crime scenes, 27, 30, 32, 109
Crimewatch TV series, 53
Criminal Investigation Department (CID), 2
criminal investigation, definitions of, 18
Criminal Justice Act (CJA, 2003), 96
Criminal Justice and Court Services Act (2000), 119
Criminal Justice and Public Order Act (CJPOA, 1994), 91, 94
Criminal Procedures and Investigation Act (CPIA, 1996), 8, 18, 22, 26, 40, 157, 180
criminal profiling, 117
critical incidents, 147–50
  criticality matrix, 148, 149
  use of national decision model, 148

cross-examination
  and special measures, 73
Crown Prosecution Service, the (CPS), 8

'Dirty Harry' policing, 134
Dando, C, 62
Data Protection Act (2018), 28
decision-making, 20, 41–5, 174
  and critical incident management, 147
  in the Golden Hours, 32
deductive reasoning, 49
Detective Degree Holder Entry Programmes (DHEP), 14
detectives
  focus on role of, 3
  public view of, 2
  training of, 3
digital devices, examination of, 111, 180
directed surveillance, 137
disability, 71
disclosure, 177, 179
dishonesty test, 136
DiYanni, R, 100
DNA evidence, 30
Domestic Violence, Crime and Victims Act (2004), 77
Dunne, S, 157
Dunninghan, C, 92

Eck, J E, 10, 166
elimination, of suspects, 58
emotional intelligence, 31
enquiries, and recommendations, 172, 173, 175

Equality Act (2010), 115
ethical dilemmas, 41
evaluation, 20, 47, 167
evidence
    Achieving Best Evidence (ABE), 70, 122
    and special measures, 69
    preservation of, 27, 28, 30, 31–2, 40
    witness statements, 64
examination, three phases of, 19
experts, drawing on, 108, 109
    examples, 120
    examples of issues with, 123
external communications, 152, 155–9

facial recognition technology, 114, 128
failure, attention on, 165
families, engaging with, 28
Feist, A, 156, 157
Ferraro, K, 35
fictional investigators, 2, 3, 26, 49, 117, 152, 164
financial investigators, 110
fingerprint analysis, 108
Fleming, J, 120
Foot, Philippa, 41
forensic archaeologists, working with, 109

Galton, Sir Francis, 108
General Data Protection Regulations (GDPR), 28
Gill, P, 166
Gillespie, M, 13
golden hour principles, 23–9, 148

Good Friday Agreement, 172
Greenwood, Paul, 179
Griffiths, A, 171
Grinshteyn, E G, 34
Guildford Four enquiry, the (1975), 3, 8, 84

Hancock, V, 37
heuristics, use of, 21
higher education, partnerships, 5
history, of policing, 2, 3
Hollywood effect, the, 164
Home Office Large Major Enquiry System (HOLMES), 8, 58
Horwell, Richard (QC), 179
House to House (H2H) strategies, 50–2
Human Rights Act (1998), 8, 43, 115, 128, 129, 130
hypothesising, 47–9

identifications, 153
IIMARCH briefing model, 33, 152, 153
incapacity, of witnesses, 71
Independent Office for Police Conduct (IOPC), 175
inductive reasoning, 49
inferences, 47–9
information
    for families and communities, 28, 78
    in the golden hours, 33
    limits of, 148
    obtained through surveillance, 139
    provided to public, 157
    sensitive and highly sensitive, 178

information, analysis of, 10, 18, 22, 40
Innes, M, 18, 26, 30, 40, 42, 47, 150, 158, 166
inspections, 167
intelligence, 30–1
    community intelligence, 113
intelligence, and proactive investigation, 22
intermediaries, use of, 73
internal communications, 152
interpreters, use of, 77
interviews and interviewing, 98
    conversation management model, 100–3
    funnel, 99
    history of, 84
    importance of, 103
    length of, 87
    PEACE model, 88
    principles of, 85–6
    process, 101
intoxication, of witnesses, 65
intrusive surveillance, 138
investigative mindset, 8, 18–20, 47, 86
Investigatory Powers Act (2016), 111
Irving, B, 92

justice system, the, 8

Kelling, G L, 63
Kerslake Report, the, 156
Klockars, C B, 134
knowledge decisions, 42

Lawrence, Stephen, death of, 2, 134, 148, 171
leadership, 33
learning disability, 71, 72
LEASH mnemonic, 50
LEAVERS mnemonic, 51
Lefkowitz, J, 174
legal decisions, 43
legislation
　facial recognition, 115
　importance of caution, 92
　important of context and evolution of, 8–9
　in historical training, 5
　influence of, 5
　keys for investigative setting, 7
Leveson Enquiry, the, 53, 157
lines of enquiry, 20, 23, 40, 47, 180
lines of responsibility, 33
Lister, S, 117
Loftus, E F, 31, 98
logistic decisions, 43
logs, keeping, 27

Macpherson report, the, 147, 165, 171
Major Incident Room Standardised Administration Procedures (MIRSAP), 58
Management of Police Information (MOPI), 172
Maras, K, 132
Mark, Sir Robert, corruption probe of, 3
Marsh, I, 106
material, attrition of, 40
Mawby, R C, 158
McLaughlin, E, 13
media
　engaging with, 53–4, 156
　role of, 13, 28
Melville, G, 106
memorandums of understanding (MOU), 119
memory, reliability of, 31, 40
Metropolitan Police, the, 10, 128
misconduct, 96
missing people, managing searches for, 109
mnemonics
　ADVOKATE, 7
　CIAPOAR, 44
　CLAD, 29
　LEASH, 50
　LEAVERS, 51
　PEACE (interviews), 87–90
　PLAN, 136
　TED PIE, 99, 100
mobile phones, examination of, 111, 180
monitoring
　of social media, 113
moral panic, 148, 169
multi-agency investigations, 119, 152, 155
Multi-agency Public Protection Arrangements (MAPPA), 119
Murder Investigation Manual (MIM), 4, 14, 117
Myhill, A, 28

National Crime Agency (NCA), 121
National Crime Recording Standards, 11
National Decision Model (NDM), 21, 43, 154, 168
　five stages of, 44
National Intelligence Model (NIM), 31
National Police Improvement Agency (NPIA, 2009), 9
naturalistic decision making, 42
necessity criteria, 133
negligence, 43
Newburn, T, 20
Neyroud, P, 8, 128, 133, 168

observation, 174
Operation Fincham, mismanagement of, 109
Operation Yewtree, 166
opinion, evidence of, 122
orality, of witnesses, 64
　conflict with special measures, 70
Ormerod, T C, 62
Osman warnings, 132
Oxburgh, G, 103

'points to prove', 6
Palmer, J C, 31, 98
Patten report, the, 171
PEACE mnemonic (interviews), 87–90
personal statement, 78
Pigot Report, the, 139
Pina-Sanchez, J, 117
PIP. see Professionalising Investigation Programme (PIP)
PLAN mnemonic, 136
Police and Criminal Evidence Act (PACE, 1984), 3, 8, 26, 28, 59, 84, 91, 92, 93, 153, 169

Police Crime Sentencing and Courts Bill (2021), 13
Police Education Qualifications Framework (PEQF), 5, 14
Police Effectiveness, Efficiency and Legitimacy (PEEL), 167
Police Search Advisors (POLSA), 108
policing. see also College of Policing
  criminal investigation as core in, 2
  history of, 2, 3
  Neyroud's cycles of, 8
policy decisions, 42
Practice Advice on Core Investigative Doctrine (CD), 3, 4
prejudice in investigative process, 8
privacy, 54, 115, 128, 139
proactive investigations, 22
probing, in interviews, 102
Proceeds of Crime Act (2002), 110
Professionalising Investigation Programme (PIP), 3, 4–5
  four levels of, 4
profiling, 117, 158
proportionality, 135–6
prosecution, 78
public
  views of policing, 2, 148, 164
  working with, 31, 155, 174

questioning techniques, 31, 32, 51, 86, 98, see also interviews and interviewing

racism, 171
Rand Corporation, the, 12
reactive investigations, 22
reasonable, use of term, 136, 180
reasoning, 49, 174
records
  keeping effective, 11, 20, 27, 78, 179
  retention periods of, 28
reflective practice
  asking questions, 85, 100
  complex cases and volume crime, 147
  fear of crime, 13
  financial investigation, 110
  information appeal, 159
  making decisions, 45
  PEACE model, 90
  personal motivation, 164
  special measures, 70
  the caution, 92
  using CHIS, 142
  volume crime, 11
Regulation of Investigatory Powers Act (RIPA, 2000), 8, 111, 115, 129, 131, 132
reliability, of witnesses, 75–6
research
  body-worn video (BWV), 117
  memory skills, 66
  statistics and effectiveness, 166
  witness credibility, 77
Rhodes, R A W, 120
Richard, Sir Cliff, 157
risk management, in critical incidents, 148, 149
Roberts, P, 18

Ross, Nick, 181
Rossmo, D K, 166
Rousseau, J J, 128
Royal Commission on Criminal Justice report, 169, 175
Royal Ulster Constabulary (RUC), 172

SAFCOM communications model, 152, 153
Sarah's Law, 96
satisficing, 21, 42, 46
Saunders, Alison, 180
Scarman report, the, 8, 169
scenes, 24, 27, 30, 32
science, of criminal investigation, 2
screening approaches, 9–10
search advisors, 108
searching powers, 29
seizure of property, 29
  return of, 78
Senior Investigating Officers (SIOs), 5, 45, 154
sensitive and highly sensitive material, 178
Shepherd, Jonathan, 31, 103
significant statements, 93
silence, right to, 91, 102
Simon, H A, 49
skills, 5
Smith, Dame Janet, 22
Smith, R G, 25
social impairment, 71
social media, 28, 31, 53, 113, 156
Speaking up for Justice report, 70
Special Branch, 2
special measures, 69–75
special warnings, 94

specialisms, drawing on, 108, 109
examples, 120
Starmer, K, 135
statistics, of crime, 11–12, 165
measuring success by, 166
Stelfox, P, 52, 97
stop and search, 8, 29, 128, 136, 169
storytelling, as communication, 156
success, 165, 167
summaries, in interviewing, 100
support services, referral to, 78
surveillance, 128, 129, 131, 135, 137–9
suspects, 26, 59–60
eliminating, 58

TED PIE mnemonic, 98, 100
testifying, fear about, 71
Theft Act (1968), 6
Thomas, Richard, 129
TIE strategies. see Trace, Interview, Eliminate (TIE) strategies
Tomlinson, M, 171
topics, in interviews, 101
Trace, Interview, Eliminate (TIE) strategies, 55–8
traditional decision making, 42
training, historical unstructured approach to, 3, 5
trauma, 31, 65
trolley problem, the, 41
'Turnbull rules', 7
Tversky, A, 21
Tyler, T R, 164

uncertainty, reduction of, 47

Victim Code (2020), victims, 10
victims, 24, 32, 174
12 rights of (Code of Practice), 77–9
support and special measures for, 69
Victim Code (2020), 77
victim satisfaction, 10
video-recorded evidence (VRE), 69, 71
volume crime, 26
definition, 9
Volume Crime Management Model (VCMM), 9–10, 146
vulnerable and intimidated witnesses, 67–75
and cross-examination, 74
identification of, 74
use of intermediaries, 73

Waldron, J, 129
West, Fred and Rose, 158
Williamson, T, 118
Wilson, J Q, 63
Winthroping, 109, 122
witnesses, 27, 32
avoiding assumptions about, 74
first account from, 64–6
importance of special measures, 71
reliability and credibility of, 75–6
vulnerabilities of, 67–6
witnesses, working with, 19
Worboys, John, 43
Wright, M, 111, 115

Yorkshire Ripper case, the, 8, 55, 58, 152, 169
Youth Justice and Criminal Evidence Act (YCEA, 1999), 69, 70, 71